Sob Stories

By Kathleen LaRocque Satullo

ZoneFree Publishing

Dedicated to
Rocky and Linda

Acknowledgements

Thank you to my family, Sandy Satullo, son Frank
Rocco, and daughter Linda Marie. You have always
been so supportive of me and my endeavors. Thank
you to my many friends who reviewed the stories and
encouraged me. And thank you to Aloma Arp for her
patience in reading each story checking for each period
and comma.

Sob Stories
Copyright © 2008 by Kathleen Satullo
Published by ZoneFree Publishing in Middletown, Ohio

ISBN 978-0-9724030-5-4
Printed in the United States of America

Cover design by Michael A. DeGiuseppe
Front Cover Photography by William Barlock
Back Cover photography by Jaryn Marie Lindner

ZoneFree Publishing
6358 Castle Hill Dr., Suite #210
Middletown, OH 45044

Contents

Introduction

Who knows what sadness
Lies inside
That smiling person
By my side.

A loss of child?
Painful heart?
Or pure loneliness?
Crying out!

That pristine tear
Shall soon appear
And cleanse the soul
Of all its fear.

- Kathleen LaRocque Satullo

After the long day, perhaps a brief respite, a short story, will immerse you in the wonderment of life. Did someone shove you today? Were you the butt of a joke? Did you stub your toe? Perhaps, dear reader, as you read some 'Sob Stories' you will come to appreciate all that you do have, even if your day wasn't perfect. Do not pass by a single face in the crowd without knowing that each person **is** a story.

Mike's Decision

I was alone in the real estate office after-hours, working on some paperwork. When the phone rang, I considered it a minor irritation. The caller said,

"Hello, this is Mike Turner, and I'm looking for information on selling my home."

WOW! This was definitely not a minor irritation. This was now pressing business. How often real estate agents sat "floor time" just looking for that elusive lead call, and here was one smack in my face.

Mike continued, "When I called ABC Realty, they said that they were Number One. Then I called XYZ Realty, and they said they were Number One. I'm confused."

I laughed into the phone and responded,

"Mike, I could say that we're Number 1. Statistics can be used so many ways. Are they Number One in a given hour on a given day in a particular area?"

So then I proceeded to educate Mike on the wherewithals of real estate. When I finished, Mike was enthusiastically impressed.

"Kathy, you've accomplished more just now than all the others. When I'm ready to list my home, I'm working with you."

We exchanged details, property address, phone numbers, etc., and Mike promised to call as soon as he ironed out some details, like a live-in girlfriend of several years. They were encountering troubles in their relationship and that was the reason for putting the house on the market. It looked like the end for them, but Mike told me he was going to do everything to try to work it out. Of course, I didn't push. He needed to sort things out without the pressure of a real estate agent, to boot.

About a month went by with no word from Mike. I called once to follow up, but he was definitely in a quandary about his future. Then, I did receive another call. This time, Mike was ready for my visit to his property to set the value. I came armed with camera, paperwork, signage, and a comprehensive property analysis. Mike was quite some specimen. Great athletic toned body, the clearest blue eyes that would rival even Paul Newman's, and just a really nice guy.

Everything went well as we went from room to room. Mike was quick to point out the fine decorating details that his girlfriend had done. She was not there, so of course I did not meet her. Unfortunately, this was yet another failed relationship, as we so often encounter in real estate. How many times did I sell a house to a nice couple, only to get a call several years later to put it back on the market due to their pending divorce. At the end of my visit, Mike still held off. He reaffirmed, "Kathy, I'm going to make one more effort to keep everything together." So I left Mike to his thoughts and waited for him to accept the final demise of his relationship.

Finally, the big decision was made and Mike invited me over. He signed all the necessary paperwork. I put the sign in the yard and when I got back to the office I got all the ads ready, downloaded all the pictures, made great flyers, brochures, and postcards – all ready to promote the property.

I went to the house the next day but no one was home, so I left my brochures in Mike's kitchen door. I tried calling him but he didn't return my call. Well, I knew he was busy with his job and since I had a key to the property, I just carried on. Days 1 and 2 and 3 passed. Soon, I did get a call from another Realtor® asking permission to show the property. Also, strangely, I got a call from Mike's mother. Now **that** was unusual. The gist of her call was to tell me that "Mike is having a really difficult time." Well, of course! It's not easy to lose your loved one and change the direction of our life. I didn't know the details of his breakup, but anyone who has lived any length of time certainly knows the pain and heartache of a lost love.

Just seven days after I listed the property, I went into the office and everyone was talking about the tragedy that had just occurred. It was in all the local news bulletins.

This ordinarily wonderful guy, Mike, just couldn't deal with his heartache. Apparently, he woke up that morning with a mission he was compelled to carry out. In his befuddled mind, the loss of his girlfriend overtook any reasonable thought in his head. He took to his car as an instrument of destruction. Running the country roads, knowing her route each day, he came upon her driving to work and he hit the gas pedal. He rammed her car, not just once, but several times. Repeatedly, over the next several miles, he pursued her and continued to bash the back end of her car Fortunately, she was able to maintain control, barely, and stayed on the road. This went on for what seemed forever, as the panicked girl tried to elude Mike's fury and rage. Concerned motorists were able to contact local police. Soon, a wild car chase ensued, with patrol cars closing in on Mike. They maneuvered in behind Mike's car, while the girlfriend pulled hard right to get off the road. The police were able to take control of the situation and continued the chase.

Soon, it was obvious to Mike he had nowhere to go. He plunged down a deep gulch separating the road from a rural parking lot, screeched on his brakes, and exited his car. Never had a man looked so desperate. His eyes were haggard and his face was puffy. His body weaved pathetically, leaning first in one direction, than another. It appeared as if he was repeating something, over and over, just lost in a fog. And then, as quickly as you can snap your fingers together, Mike pulled a gun and shot himself right through the temple. Fell to the ground, dead. Just like that! His limp body lay there, and he was gone – just gone forever.

Oh, the loss of a human being – and right in the prime of life. All for a heartache he just couldn't handle. Thank God the girl was all right. Only Mike was gone, and with such utter finality. There would be no second chance, no time to re-think his decision, no time to forge ahead with a new future. No, there would be no future at all, now.

I attended the funeral. I witnessed the mother's utter sorrow. We held onto each other in our tears – in our mother's tears, for the terrible, tragic loss. And I cried and cried for all that a mother holds in her heart for her children.

Young Love, First Love

I'll never forget two young lovers I knew back in the late 1970's. At the time, I worked in the sleepy little town of Avon, Ohio. The company I worked for was right out there in the middle of nowhere. Lots and lots of land surrounding the building, but not much of anything else. The farmers hadn't yet sold their vast tracts of acreage to the eager property developers. Urban development was still years away.

We were a close knit group, both in the office and out in the manufacturing area. Most of us had been there for years. Eventually the company grew until we needed a new, larger building, and one was built right next door. Soon, too, we needed more people – especially out in the plant. We hired an especially likeable young man, Ned Janda, just turned 18, and eager to work at the same place as his older brother. At about the same time, a young, ethereal, petite girl of about 16 popped into the office, and literally charmed her way into a position we didn't even have!! She convinced us we needed a part-time worker in the office, and that she was the one to do it! My boss instructed me to put her on the payroll.

Bonnie was that rare find – a charismatic girl who won over our hearts immediately. Her eagerness in helping out showed up at every turn. Her sheer love of life, her appreciation of the world around her, her desire to prove her self-worth, all of this entwined in this slip of a girl, made for a very happy office, indeed.

Bonnie's background was never clear to me. I only knew she was a self-made person. No real father to look over her. A mother who didn't play an important part in her life. One person did stand out, though. Her older sister. Somehow, somewhere, along the way, this was the one person who taught Bonnie to take her place in life, who instilled in her so many wonderful qualities. Bonnie had images of a world far away, of feats to be accomplished, of endless opportunities, and she would not be denied.

Ned, on the other hand, was a regular hometown boy. His roots ran deep, and his home and family life were paramount. His older brother had secured this job for him and he joyously showed up for work day after day. He enjoyed his life and was content to go along at his own pace, sure that he would find someone to share the future with him. For now, as long as he could travel the back roads and lesser used trails on his motocross bike, he was more than content. The feeling of the wind against his face, and the tree limbs slapping against his bike made his heart sing.

Time worked its magic, and soon Ned and Bonnie found each other. Two kids with bright faces, young and active, excited about life itself - just finding and discovering so much that the world had to offer. Invincible! Indestructible! One day as I looked over the 2nd floor railing to the lobby

11

below, there they were, Bonnie nestled in Ned's lap, just relishing being together. I couldn't discipline them! No one else was around, and their cuddling wasn't hurting anyone. It actually brought a smile to my face, just remembering what it was like to be young and in love.

But, change is constant. And so, too, with young lovers. In early November, Bonnie decided to move to Arizona for a while to be with her sister. Bonnie had no ties to the area. She was a "self-made" kid, no real mom in her life. She had learned early to make her own way. So in late November, she was gone. Promises flew back and forth with Bonnie and Ned.

What was to become of our beautiful Bonnie? I missed her cheerful ways, her gentle laugh, her kind spirit. For the next weeks, work was dreary and dark without the bubbling laughter of Bonnie wafting through the air. Soon, we received notice. A terrible event. A terrible disaster indeed. So sudden! So unexpected! Bonnie and her sister had car trouble along a highway in Arizona. Bonnie started to exit the car, leaving her door open. In that fraction of a second, right there on the side of the highway, a car careened into the door, slamming Bonnie to the ground, ripping her life away forever. Our beautiful Bonnie, dead in the road.

And Ned? With his Bonnie gone, Ned spent every free minute out on his motocross bike, the one way he had to be alone with his thoughts.

Avon offered so many beautiful trails through the woods and Ned used every one of them. Riding would clear his head and help banish his painful thoughts of Bonnie. One chilly February morning, Ned took off but never returned. As evening approached, people searched for him. Yes, he was found eventually. Collapsed on the trail, his bike overturned, Ned lay motionless on the dirt path. Unconscious. Paralyzed for life, now. This young, healthy, handsome boy, never again to ride with the wind, never again to dance, run, work, play.

Some years later I ran into Ned. He had a smile on his face as he pushed his wheelchair to the cash register. He found the courage to deal with his new life and he found work at a drive-through beverage store. He still had his wonderful smile, his youthful eagerness. But I couldn't help thinking what might have been. All for one day out in the woods, his life was forever changed. We talked about the past. We talked about Bonnie. He told me about their final conversation. He had told her, "I'll never see you again. You'll never come back." How prophetic those words turned out to be.

Bonnie, the sweetest girl with the sweetest smile, will never realize the rewards of adulthood. Her short, fleeting life was a joy to be a part of, but now it's nevermore.

More than 30 years later, I ran into Ned one more time. Now he worked at the local Good Will

Store. Still in his wheelchair, never married, never had children. But still with a smile on his face.

And so, my friends, when you see young love, relish in the beauty of it. It is a rare and beautiful thing. It can all be gone tomorrow.

Gerald's World

The world was gray and dreary and Gerald had despaired of anything turning it around for him. Anything right here and now, anyway. Perhaps this **was** the time to move on. He certainly didn't feel like he was any kind of success story at the moment. His first marriage had ended in divorce. A second marriage proved to be even more disastrous! It sure didn't feel good to be a two-time loser at the marriage game. He knew he was a decent guy. As he sat in the dim room, he decided this was the time to just pack his bags and leave town. Leave for places unknown – start over again. Would a fresh start get him on the road to happiness? He didn't know, but what he **did** know was that inaction would only result in every day being dreary, endless, and depressing.

There was one bright spot in Gerald's life, one person who had caught his eye. But that was way back in high school, of all things. And that girl, Caryn, certainly hadn't been interested in him. Actually, she dated his best friend. So, Gerald had always looked on from afar, and could only imagine what might have been, what could be, what wasn't.

He reached in his closet and brought out his bags. Packing would keep his mind occupied. Packing would allow him to get in motion, take action, move on with his life.

Just recently he had an accidental meeting with Caryn's brother, Tim. Tim had been talkative and brought Gerald up-to-date on a thousand everyday occurrences about their families. It was a long conversation, but it only made Gerald realize how he had always cared about Caryn.

Caryn had married soon after graduation. She taught school. She had a son. These were the things Gerald knew.

So, as Gerald slowly closed his baggage, he made one final decision. He would not leave town without at least calling Caryn. So what if he hadn't seen or talked to her in years. Something inside Gerald propelled him to the telephone. Swallowing deep gulps of air, he dialed the number Tim had given him. A delightful feminine voice answered. "Hello". Gerald couldn't back down now. "Hi Caryn, this is Gerald." She actually knew his voice and seemed to encourage the conversation. Gerald talked about this and about that and about everything under the sun. He just couldn't seem to stop, because once he did, there would never be another opportunity again to have Caryn all to himself.

Finally, though, Gerald had to step aside. "Caryn, I'm sorry to keep you on the line forever. Your husband must be concerned about who you're talking to for so long."

And then the skies parted, and the stars shot through the night. Moonbeams whispered, and the trumpets blared. The crescendo of music and the beauty of the night sky swept over Gerald. Why? This is what he heard.

"Gerald, didn't you know. I divorced last year." Of all the things her brother, Tim, said to Gerald, he had left out the most important detail – Caryn was free and available!

Gerald never did leave town. He saw Caryn that very next night, and the next and the next. He had always known Caryn would be his love. But now Caryn returned that love.

Fifteen years later, here at the office we call them "The Velcro Twins" because they are just so much attached to each other. And they go on in matrimonial bliss!

The Plank and the Bull

Connie was a seasoned Realtor® who worked frequently with country properties. She was considered the office expert on farms, acreage, and land. Susie, a newer agent, had a lead on a property in the southern part of our county, but she felt ill-prepared to go on the appointment alone. She asked Connie to accompany her for the previewing of the property in order to set the right price.

They took off one sunny, summer day. Upon arrival, old farmer Jerry took them for a walk of the property. He was glad to show off his barn, his farm animals, and especially his bull. They stood back from the fence and admired the brute, stomping his feet in all his majesty.

Somehow, somewhere, something spooked Big Bull. He must have been on a sugar high anyway, because almost immediately he went into a frenzy. He started running around, racing back and forth, challenging the fence. Finally, he did get loose! The bull attacked the fence, he attacked a shed, he charged a clothesline, and then he charged the barn, most specifically a loose plank that was flapping. The bull just plain mounted the plank and started bumping and humping!

Connie and Susie had never seen anything like it! Farmer Jerry certainly didn't seem capable of handling this situation, and the bull kept roaring and snorting in his frenzy. Susie was stubborn, though, and wanted to stand her ground. She had a listing at stake, and wasn't going to be scared off. However, the situation escalated and the snorting just got louder!

Connie had had enough by this time! The farmer was yelling, the bull was snorting, Suzie was screaming yet still trying to stand her ground, and finally Connie started running, screaming into the wind, "Let's just get the f--- outta here!!" Needless to say, they didn't hang around for the listing.

Sink that Putt

Lorie was always such a poised person. She knew her stuff and was a very successful Realtor®. As such, she was showing a lovely property situated on a very large lot. The house showed beautifully, and Lorie sensed a sale in the offing.

The prospective buyers, a man, his wife, and two children, next set out to enjoy the wide open spaces in the spacious yard. As they all stood there discussing the pros and cons of the property, things went very well.

A few minutes later, all parties moved to the side yard to continue their tour. At that moment, the spot right where they had been standing just **sunk** right into the ground! A sink hole! There was no backyard left!! Poised Lorie turned white as a sheet and the buyers looked absolutely sick!

They bought the property, though! They got a deal on it.

Dressed for Success

I had a great outfit – matching houndstooth shoes to go with my houndstooth suit! Really spiffy. I had it on the day I got a call on one of my vacant properties. An agent showing the property noticed that someone had used the toilet in the house, it hadn't flushed, and it was a sight to behold! The water had been turned off since the house was vacant, and I certainly couldn't let this toilet situation go unattended.

I went home, fetched a pail, and headed out to the property. There were houses all up and down the street, so I knew it wouldn't be a problem to knock on a neighbor's house to fill the pail with water to wash down the turd in the toilet. What I hadn't counted on was that it was in the middle of the day, and every door I knocked on went unanswered.

Finally, as I passed house after house after house, I finally found someone home. I was able to fill my bucket. As I walked up the middle of the street, reality really hit! Here I was in my fine houndstooth suit, and my fine houndstooth shoes, looking every bit the professional, yet trudging up a street, carrying a bucket of water, to flush a stool down the toilet!

Dog

I really liked "dog". He was affectionate, and every time I visited the property, he greeted me warmly.

Acting as the listing Realtor®, I finally sold the house, but had to stand by for several inspections. Finally, I had to be available for the gas man to come do a final reading. Since the owner was at work, I was the contact person. But I couldn't pin the gas company down as to what time of day they would be there. As I sat there in the morning, I couldn't help but think of all the other things I could be doing that day.

Taking matters into my own hands, I knocked on the next door neighbor's house and was lucky! He was home and willing to assist the gas man when he came. I was free! However, I knew I couldn't leave the dog there. That could be a problem. But 'dog' was so friendly, and he liked me so much, I knew I wouldn't have a problem with him.

I got a leash, and started leading him to my car. Right then and there I should have aborted my mission. 'Dog' was so excited to be outside that he lunged ahead. Oh yes, did I mention that 'dog' was a big dog. He pulled me right off my feet. Before I knew what happened, he had dragged me through a mud puddle, but I held on to the leash for life! Finally, I managed to get 'dog' into the front seat, and I had to admit, he looked so cute sitting there!

I went home to my beautiful fenced-in yard and thought to myself that 'dog' could spend quality time with lots of space to run and enjoy himself. As I went to pull away, I saw 'dog' charge the chain link fence, and bark incessantly at the neighbor's dog on the other side. Well, I couldn't have him disturbing the neighborhood. So what now. Quickly I thought, well, I'll put him in the garage! As I proceeded to do this, I knew it wouldn't work. I had two brand new box springs and mattresses in the garage for my kids, and I could just imagine 'dog' shredding them to pieces. What now? Oh well, I would just have to attach his leash to the base of our basketball pole. That's what I did, and when I got word about two hours later that the gas man had come and gone, I went home to fetch 'dog' and return him.

But when I got home – no dog! There was the leash, broken! Right away, it dawned on me that I had a huge liability going on here. I lost my customer's dog! I had to act fast. It didn't help that I had a woods behind my house! I posted signs immediately at the local convenient store, knocked on my neighbors' doors, and started driving up and down streets looking for 'dog'. I must have gone up and down the streets for over a half-hour when finally I saw my next door neighbor, a good eight months' pregnant, run out into the street to flag me down. She was out of breath, but she was able to shout out, "Kathy, I saw the dog come padding right down the middle of the street and I was able to run out and grab him and I put him in my backyard!" What great news for me! What a great neighbor!

I retrieved 'dog' from the backyard and plopped him in my car. As I was driving back to his house, I glanced over for a closer look at 'dog' and my heavens! He must have had a field day on his excursion through the woods and neighborhood. Feathers, and blood, and whatnot were sticking out all ends of his mouth! He must have eaten every bird, rabbit, and critter in the neighborhood! I was never so glad to get a dog home. Let the owner wonder how he got all those feathers in his mouth. I wasn't going to breathe a word.

Anna
(but no King of Siam)

Anna had tunnel vision and was probably one of the most naïve people I ever met. I asked myself, "How does one get to be 86 years old, and still be so trusting and simple.

Anna lived in a small 2-bedroom home at the deserted end of a small, dusty road. Her husband had died many years earlier, so she lived there all alone. Her only son lived about 40 miles away, with his wife Brunhilde. They firmly believed it was time for Anna to give up her independence and come live with them. They were adding a room onto their house just for her.

That's when I entered the picture. I had sent fliers to that area, announcing my status as a Realtor®, albeit a newer one, and asking for business. When I met with Anna, she had my flyer clutched in her gnarled hands, and we set about the task of filling out paperwork. I'm not sure how her tunnel vision worked – but she saw enough to sign in the correct spots. I explained how property values were appreciating – and that even her modest, small home could fetch about $60,000.

Soon, we had our first showing. My phone rang at the office. It was the agent showing the property. He was talking very fast and he sounded very nervous. "Slow down," I said. "Now, please explain the problem."

He was a newer agent. He blurted out, "I don't know what I should do. As I was showing my customer the house, my customer asked straight out to Anna – how much would you take for the house? And she said $30,000!"

I simply told the agent to have no further dialog with Anna, and to instruct his customer to have no further conversation with her, too. After they left the property, I got in my car and drove over to talk to Anna. I asked, "Anna, why would you say you would take $30,000 for your house when it's worth almost $60,000?"

"Vell, Kat-tee, you know, von of ta last tings my husband tol' me before he died vas dat if I ever had to sell da house – "Don't take a penny less den $30,000." Whoa….that was over 15 years ago. Next, I called the family and told them what happened. Brunhilde made sure to call Anna and in strong, harsh words instructed her to keep quiet when potential buyers were going through the house. In other words, keep your mouth shut!

Okay, we got another request for a showing. So, I called Anna. I could hear her weak, trembling voice on the other end of the line. "I know, Kat-tee, I no 'lowed to speak ven pipple here." I felt so bad for Anna. But wouldn't you know it, she did speak! This time she promised the buyers she would put siding on the little back room addition. And, they did make an offer on the property, along with the stipulation that the siding was included in the offer price.

Anna was way too naïve and innocent to negotiate for the repair, so I assured the family that I could find a trusted handyman to do the job for a reasonable price. Whew! I was glad to have someone over quickly. He reported the job took twice as long because of the wasp nest tucked in the corner of the addition. He could get up about two rows of siding, then he had to run for his life as the wasps attacked. When they settled down, he could do a little more, and so on, and so on, until he was done.

Finally the day came for the trip to the bank to sign closing paperwork. Again, I assured the family that I would pick Anna up and bring her, thereby saving them quite a trip since they lived in the opposite direction. I knew something was up right away. Anna got in my car, and she had a rather purposeful look on her face. As I gathered speed, I felt a little nudge in my side. Anna poked me, "Kat-tee, dis is for you." As I glanced over, I saw she was pushing a white envelope into my lap. I panicked! I sensed that there was money in that envelope! I said, "Anna, you know that by selling your house I earned a commission. I made money. If there's money in that envelope, I certainly can't take it." And, I repeated, "I made a commission on selling your house."

Everything went smoothly at the bank, and the family even bought me a lovely gift. They felt that I had certainly gone over and above what most Realtors® would do and that I had taken extra, special, care of Anna. We all parted ways afterward, and I drove Anna home. As I drove, I speculated about Anna's future life. I just felt that Anna was old and meek, and it seemed such a shame to shut her up in Brunhilde's house. I knew Anna would never have a moment's peace there, or any independence. Brunhilde was a forceful, blunt person – and I feared that Anna would be forever a silent member of the household.

I took Anna home and reluctantly let her out of the car. In some small measure, I felt like I was deserting her. She looked like such a lonely little woman walking up the walkway to her door. We waved goodbye and I headed to the office. As I drove, I saw a little piece of white poking up from the crevice in the passenger seat. Oh no! Anna had tucked her little envelope in my car! I panicked. I couldn't take money! But, was it money in the envelope. Maybe I had nothing to worry about. I sped to the office to confer with my manager. However, when I arrived, she wasn't there. I stood there with the envelope, nervously debating whether I should open it or not. But, another agent confidently took the problem into her own hands, and with one sure swoop of her hand, ripped open the envelope. Ohmigosh! What should fall out but three one hundred dollar bills. I was shocked!

It seemed like the longest hour in my life, until my manager came in. "Oh, Kathy, that's okay to be bonused by the owner of the home. It's the buyer you don't want to take anything from." So I

was free to keep the money. But I still felt a
nagging feeling going on in my head. That evening,
I called Brunhilde and told her the facts of the day.
Big, booming, Brunhilde – the boss of a family if
you ever saw one – responded, "Oh, Kathy. We
knew Anna wanted to give you something. We
knew about the money. She must have really liked
you because she has never done anything like that
before."

Well, I tucked another sale in my belt. But I
have often wondered how things worked out with
Anna and Brunhilde. Our lives touched briefly, yet
Anna taught me so much about old age and
believing and trusting in the world as we know it. I
will never forget Anna.

Hospital Stay

Dave Lloyd woke up to a frightful sight! While showering, he noticed an awful blotch of discoloration covering his entire upper leg. Web-like strands took on a veiny appearance as they wove their way in an ever-widening circle about his thigh. Dave was 72-years old and in great shape. He had worked hard to maintain his health and energy and it showed. He was the "quick wit" in the office, and always had a gleam in his eyes. He may have been 72, but inside he was that scheming 16-year old. As a matter of fact, we had taken to calling him "Bad Boy Lloyd." But now, he looked like he was in for a very bad time.

Hurriedly, he called for his wife, Sarah. She came racing into the bathroom. They both just stared and stared at this horrible affliction. Was it a circulation problem? Was there a blockage somewhere in the body causing it? Was this a life-threatening situation. They decided at once that Sarah would have to drive Dave to the emergency room. This couldn't wait!

The two of them barreled into the emergency room, stating Dave needed immediate attention. Quickly, the nurse on duty put Dave into a private station area, instructing him to immediately remove his trousers and put on a hospital gown. While Dave did this, Sarah shared more information with the nurse. The nurse then entered the curtained area to inspect Dave's leg. She looked down closely – and then more closely. Finally, she continued to stare at the huge discoloration, and murmured "Oh my God!" Dave did a quick intake of breath. The nurse continued, "I think that's ballpoint ink!" At once, Dave, Sarah, and the nurse all closed in for the closest inspection, yet. And omigosh!! It **was** ballpoint ink. Apparently, the night before, Dave had come home and thrown on an old pair of pants – not aware that a "leaker" ballpoint pen was in the pocket!!!

Dave laughed and laughed and laughed – and said "It's a good thing I didn't come in here limping, or worse from the power of suggestion, think that I was dying!" And even though Dave, Sarah, and the nurse all had a good laugh, Dave was sure he was the talk of the hospital once he exited!

The Fat Lady Sings

We all noticed her, but we never talked to her.
Thank goodness we were never intentionally cruel
to her, but she sure didn't fit in with our group – or
anyone else's group. No one ever extended a hand
to her in friendship, or to make her feel accepted.
No, she would never share in with our whispered
conversations during class, nor our weekend plans.
She was forever the fat girl, the one with the pimply
face and greasy hair. We basically just ignored her.
Especially during gym class. We would all prance
out in those traditional, awful, blue bloomer type
one-piece gym outfits. Nothing here to show off
your figure, but plenty to make you look downright
dowdy! And there was "fat girl". She, more than
anyone else, looked so pathetic. Her dimpled,
folded, gobs of fat would hang off her arms and
legs. Her tummy and butt would burst at the
seams. Her lumbering weight would stop her from
ever running, jumping, or leaping, as was required
in gym.

Now, of course, during the semester, we all
had to perform on the "horse". We needed big,
strong strides to gather momentum for the giant
leap in the air. Then, over-over-over the horse, and
the wonderful, clear shot to the other side. It was
fun and we enjoyed this session of gym class. But
wait, what about "fat girl". We would all be
dreaming to think she would ever even get up
enough momentum, or height, to come anywhere
close to accomplishing this task. We would all
stand, with bated breath, watching her lumbering

gait, onward and onward to that fateful horse. We all knew there was **no chance** she would clear it. She never, ever, even tried. She knew it was an impossible task. So, how did she perform. She would start her painful lumbering gait, step by step, with the whole class watching. She would keep up that awful gait, right up to the horse, and then just ram right into it – with no effort whatsoever to heave her enormous body over to the other side. No, we didn't make fun of her, but as her body got closer, and ever closer to the horse, we all knew she would run into it with her giant belly. And, just at the moment of impact, the whole class grunted as one - "Ooooomph"- more in sympathy with her at the impact, than for any other reason.

However, thoughts of this gym class have stayed with me a lifetime. I always remember this lonely, shell of a girl. We didn't stop once to give her the time of day. How lonely her high school years must have been. How absolutely dreadful. And whenever I look back, I wish I could have been the one to extend a hand, or even a quick "hi", if even for a brief moment. It would have been such a simple thing to do, and it might have brightened her day – if only for a moment.

One Moment in Time

We were sitting on the sofa watching television. I had known you for only 37 days, but I felt so comfortable with you. You had a great sense of integrity and honesty, a wonderful laugh, a soft demeanor. I found all this to be very attractive. We had biked through the Metro Parks, walked along forest trails, went out on the pier to see the reddest sunset ever, even played cards together. We had shared such great conversations and such innocent dates, which gave me a chance to get to know you without the distractions of romantic interludes.

However, this very fact – that we had not even touched or kissed - was bringing about some rare feelings inside my body. There had always only been my husband. Since my separation and divorce, I had not had any sexual activity. I even swore to myself that I didn't need anyone. That was all past. It was just me from now on, and I could function very well for myself, thank you. But earlier this day, whenever I thought of you, I felt strong sensations and urges within my own body that I couldn't deny. Every time I would think of you, and your kindness and easygoing nature, I would start to envision being with you totally. This was incredible to me. I couldn't believe I was having these thoughts.

So, as you and I sat on the sofa, eventually you did lean over and ever so nicely kiss me. Then, you kept kissing me and it felt wonderful. I just loved it! I have always been self-conscious of my kissing because I think I'm a very inexperienced kisser. But you kissed so wonderfully that I felt myself responding and not feeling all that bad about any shortcomings I might have. I was enjoying just being held and kissed, and this went on a while. Then, you asked me, "What are you thinking right now?"

I just had to be truthful when I answered, "I'm thinking that I had strong desires today, feelings in my body." Then I added, "I am going to be with you, but not tonight. I'm scared. I want to be with you, but I'm scared."

You didn't make demands, or force the issue. You were just so perfect in your response. We just kissed more, and I actually wanted you to put your hands all over my body. I couldn't bring myself to actually say that to you, but I was hoping so hard that you would touch me intimately, everywhere. Finally, I looked up at you and said, "And what are you thinking right now?" You replied, "Well, actually the same thing you were thinking before."

Already, earlier that day, I had accepted in my mind that I wanted to be intimate with you, but of course I was afraid. In my whole life, I had known only one man. This was all so new to me. I had to sort out what I was feeling. But, deep down, I knew that I wanted you to make love to me.

I asked you if you wanted to go into my bedroom. We ended up by the side of the bed and

I was feeling timid and frightened. I put my hands up to cover my eyes, as if I could hide from the whole situation. I told you, "I won't watch you," as you were undressing. Then, I lay down on the bed and you were beside me. You were very gentle and kind, just kissing me, and then caressing me. It felt so good. Your kisses were sweet, and you kissed my lower lip, and ever so slightly explored my mouth. These sensual feelings aroused me as I thought I could never be aroused. When our bodies finally met, I loved it. It was the most wonderful, tender, sexual experience I have ever had.

Afterwards, as we lay on the bed, our bodies still entwined, I felt fulfilled. I will never regret this experience. It was one of the nicest moments in my life.

Becky

Becky had a most challenging job during her college years. Since she was working towards a teaching degree, specializing in the education of physically and mentally challenged young children, she felt it was right in line to take a position with a nursing home – one that specialized in the elderly challenged. To be sure, she had to remember who took what medications, and when, and how much. She was a sweet, tender voice in many of their daily lives. Becky was all of nineteen years old, just a fresh faced youth herself. She bathed them with care, she made attempts to teach them some very basic skills, but it was much too late to reach most of them. She tried, though.

Once in a while, an excursion was planned. What a delight to get these elderly, confused patients out in the sunshine, on a nice, planned agenda. And so it was one day when the buses pulled up and Becky, along with three other caregivers, loaded the forty or so patients for a sunny day visiting one of the lovely nature centers in the area.

Some of the patients were childlike with wonder at the sights and sounds they were enjoying. Becky and the caregivers loved moments like this, when despite all odds, their patients could feel the freedom of a life outside of the home. The day ended all too soon, and everyone loaded the buses for the trip back. Cruising down the highway at a moderate speed, the buses took care to stay together. No chances were taken – safety was of the utmost importance.

But just when the hum of the wheels almost put everyone to sleep, Becky felt a bump, bump, bump – and then a dead stop. Omigosh! The bus had a flat tire! Now, both buses were pulled over to the shoulder of the highway. No such things as cell phones.....no quick fix! By now it was late in the day and very soon almost all these patients would be due for their medications. Medications to keep them calm, to keep them focused, to keep them from wandering off, to help maintain their persona. What in the world am I going to do with a busload of elderly, mentally challenged patients out here on the side of the highway, Becky thought! While the other bus continued on to send help back, Becky led her group in song. She became challenged herself, as she continually tried to think of ways to divert their attention and stave off their thoughts or needs for medications. She pulled out every trick in the book, games and songs she had long ago abandoned. She didn't even want to think what people in the passing cars might be thinking of this strange sight – a disabled bus, with a bunch of old people standing around, singing!

Finally, help arrived. Inside, Becky felt like collapsing. She had pulled it off. Everyone arrived home no worse for wear or tear! But this encounter never paled in Becky's memory. It served her well for graduation and then her real job, working day in and day out with an entire classroom of mentally challenged children – the ones that used to be "shunned" by society. Her rewards have been many – and her unending patience and caring have made many young lives brighter and happier than they otherwise might have been. Thank goodness there are dedicated young students who have taken on the responsibility to ensure that special care is given to those with special needs!

Cracker

Email
Fri, 10 Dec 2004
Subject: My Pet Cracker
Hi Chris,
Just writing for one purpose only. To tell you about my cat, Cracker.

Chris, it's like re-living the whole process of when mom got weaker and weaker, day by day, with the cancer.

The vet can't tell me exactly what's wrong with my cat. That would cost $250 for diagnostic, another $250 for blood work, which could indicate an operation for about $500, and even at that, it could be cancer and she would die anyway.

But, all in all, every day she just withers to skin and bones. I come home from work and she's laying in the same spot that I left her. I'm so afraid each day that that will be the day that I come home and she just doesn't move anymore. She looks at me with her helpless eyes and I snuggle her, and kiss her. I tell her that I love her   Just about every night I sob. I pick her up very gently and always put her on my bed because she looks so beautiful and comfortable there. When I pick her up, she feels like a feather. She used to be almost 12#. I don't even want to know what she weighs now.

I know there's a big difference between a person and a pet…but it just brings back memories of mom's failing days so much. Now I'm watching my dear pet of nine years go through this. I know I'll be a basket case on the day I finally come home and she's in her eternal sleep. It's just that I've always had cats, and this has never happened with any of them. I will not put her to sleep! I would feel it was such a betrayal. But then again, if she is in pain, and I can see that, then I must. She doesn't cry, or meow, as if in pain. So, I just love her every day. It's hard to leave for work. Can you imagine her dying here all alone. But I can't stay home every day. So before I leave for work. I spend a lot of time with her, just in case it's the last time I see her alive.

I must leave for work now. Just had to write to someone who would understand the correlation between mom and Cracker - and how I might be feeling. There are so few people who would truly understand,

Love
Me.

My most beautiful, wonderful friend left me today. What an awful decision. My lovely, gentle, most loyal friend who trusted me unconditionally - gone.

When I first laid eyes on her and held her in my arms, selecting her out of her litter of kittens, she just cuddled up to me, and looked at me with the most trusting eyes in the world. I cradled her, and Sandy nodded, "yes, we'll take this one." She had a beautiful calico coat, a sweet kittenish face, and she just nestled against me for the long ride home.

On the way, I got to take a really good look at her close up. Oh my gosh! Fleas! Worse yet, the fur under her chin was eaten up - mites! And to make matters even more serious, the next day when I called her, she didn't hear me. She was deaf! What was I to do with a deaf cat? Of course, I made the vet appointment right away. I did all the necessary things for the safekeeping of my new kitty, the things any good owner would do. I had her fleas treated, along with the mites. Initial shots were given. She also had a fierce upper respiratory infection. The doctor gave me medicine to treat this ailment. However, the doctor wasn't so sure about the deafness. He took her into the dog kennel, and when he came back, he said, "Yep, she's deaf. She didn't move a muscle even when all the dogs barked!" I asked "What does that mean? A deaf cat!!" How was I to handle this? What does a deaf cat do? How do you call her in the house when you want her? How does she get along?

Sandy came through on this one. Usually pessimistic, he was the one who took hold of the situation. He bought a bell! He was convinced she could hear high pitched sounds.

So, for the next week or so, I rang the bell for her, and darned if she didn't seem to come. Somewhere along the way, she actually started coming even without the bell. When her respiratory infection medicine ran out, I thought I had figured it out. Her infection was so bad that it must have affected her in many ways, one being the temporary loss of hearing.

In the coming months, she proved to be a warm, affectionate kitty. She cuddled into the form of my body, and her warmth was soothing. One thing she never was able to do, though, was purr. I think the infection forever wiped out this ability.

She was born somewhere around the 4th of July, so we named her "Firecracker." Called her "Cracker" for short.

Cracker saw me through some tough times. She was there for me during my divorce, through helping me get my daughter settled, through the death of my mother. She was always there, allowing me to either weep, or find solace when I buried my face in her fur. She was just **there** for me....always. She soothed my frazzled nerves. I could come home all worked up, and see her lounging peacefully in a chair, or my bed, or anywhere - and immediately I could feel the tension ease out of me.

I so enjoyed seeing her outside, running with the wind, or sun bathing on a hot summer day. She was always the lady. She did have one strange habit, though, of tipping over her food bowl, preferring to eat her cat food off the floor - batting it with her paw, then chasing it, and then eating it. I got such a kick out of that.

Time goes fast, or slow, depending on what you're looking forward to. However, time just passed, day by day, month by month, year by year.

My dear, sweet Cracker only lived a short life. Just nine years. What happened? I don't know. One day she just coughed up blood. Why? I don't know. Took her to the vet and he didn't know. It would take lots of diagnostic work, plus blood work, maybe an operation, and then she could have cancer and die anyway. That's what the vet said.

I tried some medicine he gave me, and she seemed to improve. For about a week, anyway. And then the horrible deterioration began. How terribly awful to see something you love, something that depends on you, something that has been loyal to you no matter if you are a good person or bad person, slowly die. I could see the weight just melt off of her. She grew more helpless every day. Her eyes lost their alertness. But her dignity was so great, that she would weakly stagger to her litter box. It would take her three stages. She would have to stop and rest at each stage - but her will and pride enabled her to reach her box - her dignity was intact.

The last morning, I pet her and comforted her for a long time. Was I being unfair? I didn't want to let her go. The tears welled up in me and I felt such futility in that there was nothing I could do for my beloved pet. I didn't want to leave her, but I had to go to work. I didn't want her to be alone for the final moments. She could barely lift her head. I could hear a rasping from deep inside of her. Was she in pain? How would I know? What could I do? I was losing my beauty - my Cracker. Finally, I had to leave.

When I came home that night, I dreaded coming through the door, not sure what I would see. As I opened the door, there she was. She had made it to the utility room - and was lying on her side by the water bowl - it had tipped over and her side was wet from laying in it. She was too weak to even move. I toweled her off. At what point does selfishness - a selfishness to keep her alive because I wanted her alive - turn over to accepting the inevitable.

I called the vet, and sobbed uncontrollably when a voice answered. "What should I do?" I asked. "How would I know if my cat was in pain? Would she be better off at home?" The vet tried to walk me through the obvious. My cat would be free of pain, free to live forever, if I just had the guts to do it - Euthanasia.

God, how I sobbed as I swaddled her in a soft, terry towel. Her little body was so limp she felt like a rag doll. I arrived at the vet and after looking at my beloved Cracker, she gave me the ultimate choice. Waiting **would** only cause pain to my sweet friend. It must be done.

My gentle, beautiful Cracker lay there so still. Even when they injected her, she was so weak she didn't respond. I hugged her little head, and whispered into her fur, "Cracker, I love you. " I heard the vet from a long way off saying "She's gone." My most wonderful friend was gone. They were kind at the vets. We lovingly draped her body with the terry cloth towel. They helped me to the door.

It's a cold, snowy December night. There is no one with me now. I'm home. It's dark. I have my soft as can be, limp bundle cradled in my arms. I must take a shovel, and forever lose my cat to another world. I have dug a spot right outside my living room window. I want to be able to look out on a sunny day, and know she's there. Right where she used to sun herself. Right where she used to love to wile away the hours.

Cracker was my friend. She listened to me. I could talk endlessly. I could sing to her. I could babble if I wanted. I could act silly, cry, laugh, or just pet her. And she accepted me totally for who I am. She never tried to change me. I think I've lost a lot.

E-Mail
Tue, 14 Dec. 2004
Hi Kathy,
I am so sorry that you lost Cracker. There is
nothing more loving than a pet and after losing
four pets of my own, I certainly know exactly how
you feel. We have never forgotten any of our dogs
that we have lost and we never will. They were all
special. Bob and I are sorry for your loss.
Sincerely,
Marilyn

E-Mail
Tue, 14 Dec 2004
Cathy,
I'm sorry about Cracker. I had to dry my eyes
several times while reading your tribute. I feel
really sad. Cracker was a good cat. I know how
you feel. I never thought I would feel such a loss
as when Xena didn't come home. I still feel a great
loss when I think of her. I only hope that she had a
painless death. I feel your pain. Cracker and Xena
are together again. And they're happy.
Sandy

E-Mail
Tue, 14 Dec 2004
Oh Kathy,
I'm so sorry. I know how you feel. I've lost two
cats and a dog and I mourned them all for months
afterwards. It's such an awful thing to happen
during the holidays. It's hard to be happy and get
excited about the season.

My prayers are with you. Cry as much as you can now and you'll cry more even after time goes by. But think of all the happiness she brought you and that you gave to her. She had a great life with you and was very lucky and happy
Love
Cher

E-Mail
Mon, 13 Dec 2004
What a beautiful tribute to a beloved friend. You're in our thoughts.
Carla and Gary

E-Mail
Wed, 14 Dec 2004
Kathy,
Thanks for making my makeup run down my cheeks. What a beautiful scenario and so touching. This is one reason I could never have a pet. I can't say 'Good-bye'. That is a wonderful tribute to your sweet pet and friend. Thanks for sharing it.
Betty B.

E-Mail
Wed, 15 Dec 2004
Oh Betty….what kind words. Thank you so much. Yes, I miss her a lot. It might sound funny to say the house is so quiet without her (because honestly, how much noise does a cat make?), but the house **is** quiet without her. I talked to her all the time. Now my house is empty. I still have Pumpkin, but she is so independent. Her nickname is 'Ho Bag',

cause she's always going outside and meeting lord
only knows who??

The Diary

Our family met the day after my mom died, as families do at time like that. We sat and talked, and of course looked through all the old pictures and family albums. The pictures helped us recount the memorable times in my mom's life, the stories we grew up with. We talked, we cried, we reminisced. Then Chris called out, "Here it is! She still kept it." And what did Chris have in her hands? It was an old diary my mom had kept. In all my life, I never knew this book existed. It was a five-year diary with a beautiful glossy cover. I glanced through this book, and I knew I could not let it go at that. I needed to take this book home with me to discover its contents.

Later that evening, when I was all alone, I took this precious book and opened it to the first page. Written on this page were the words, "To Miss Josephine Masar. May many interesting things be put in this book."

I was about to read about my mom, not as the nurturing, caring mother I knew, but as a young, exciting girl, with all the hopes and dreams of a lifetime to look forward to. As I began to read, I was transported in time back to 1934, and my mother's life as a young, beautiful 18-year old. Each entry was so precious to me. Her wonderful expressions – like "Ye Gods and little fishes," or after a fun night, she would say, "That was swell." Entry after entry talked about dancing, dancing, and more dancing, until three in the morning most times. And all her dances were taken, by too many boys to mention here.

How she enjoyed life! She was vibrant, active, and so alive!! I could feel her spirit as I read. I could feel her frustration in trying to find a job. I could feel her disappointments, her doubts, her thoughts about who to spend the rest of her life with. Eventually, I came across her first mention of dad. Her five-year diary ends in the 4th year, with her marriage. Her entry? She says, "My wedding day, the happiest day of my life when I went up the altar to become Clifford's wife. It rained, but who cares?"

There were many, many entries in the book. Many of them I will hold close to my heart forever. Her private thoughts, her private wishes, her private dreams, and all these I will cherish forever.

Now I know why she never lectured us. She never preached. She never judged. She never threatened us. Because she knew what it was to have fun, stay out late, laugh, and dance an endless dance.

At the end, when God had taken almost everything away from mom, yet she was still able to speak, I went into her room and sat by her side. She was still able to see, and as I sat down, she said the last thing she was ever able to say to me. She said, "I don't know who you are, but you have a nice smile." How unbelievable – my mom lay there dying, she had no idea who I was, yet still found it within herself to simply say such a kind, kind thing.

Dolores

I will never forget Dolores. As a newlywed, I had
moved to a small town, had my first baby, and
money was tight. Certainly there was no extra
money for gas to visit my relatives just 15 miles
away. Heck, I didn't even have money for a dish
towel, now that we were down to a one-income
family with a baby to feed. I was going nuts! Just
me, alone, all day, with a baby. How I longed for a
decent conversation! Over the winter a house was
completed just two doors down, and a young
family moved in. But who gets to meet neighbors
in the winter! Finally, Spring! I was outside just to
get **outside**! And I met lovely Dolores. It is so
cliché to say someone is as beautiful on the inside
as they are on the outside. But this was never more
true than in Dolores. She really was beautiful, an
absolute look-alike of Audrey Hepburn.   And her
spirit? And patience? And quiet sternness with her
children? I never heard her yell! The most she
would do was clamp her jaw tight and then call out
to her children, using their middle names. They
knew they were in trouble.

Over the next five years, we became such
good friends. We shared parenting techniques and
home decorating ideas. But most importantly, we
were just there for each other. One day I would
walk over and visit at her house. The next day she
would come down to my house. Our children
played together so well, and they became little
friends, too.   To be honest, I don't know what I
would have done without this friendship. The

winters weren't so isolated. I didn't have to worry about driving into Cleveland to visit friends. Fight with the husband? I had someone to stress out with. Trouble with the kids? A friend to suggest ideas. Back and forth, back and forth, visiting. In summers, we enjoyed going out in the fields behind our houses to pick blueberries with the kids. In the fall, time for raking leaves and letting the kids jump in. Ordinary activities, but they filled the days with fun and laughter and solid friendship.

One awful incident did occur, which only bespoke of the kindness of this dear lady. Dolores and her family had just returned from a fantastic trip out west using their motor home. Along the way, she picked up a delicate and treasured piece of china. It was beautiful, sitting there in her living room. We admired it no end. Our kids played and laughed in the living room, while we went into the kitchen for coffee. Just then, unbelievably, the inevitable crash! My young daughter, of all people, had accidentally knocked over this lovely piece of china and it lay there in a million shattered pieces. I was mortified. How in the world could I make this up to Dolores. Oh! How amazing this woman was! No sign of what she must be feeling inside. Her expensive piece was ruined beyond belief, and yet she uttered no word to add to my horror and grief! I did try to replace the item, but she wouldn't hear of it.

Change is constant, true in all situations. When my youngest turned five and started school, I made the decision to go back to work. How subtly we build new worlds for ourselves. No longer did I have that leisure time to visit with an old friend. Weekdays were spent packing up the kids for the babysitter, getting to work, fitting all the ordinary things into an extra tight schedule. Weekends were spent grocery shopping, cleaning house. Just not much time for a friendly cup of coffee in anyone's kitchen. It took a long time, but soon the "hi's" across the yard were less and less. Dolores, too, took a job at the local school, tending to the schoolchildren at recess.

The friendship would always be there. But the daily rituals had definitely come to a standstill.

Years went by. My son and daughter graduated high school. Then off to college for them. About this time, a brief encounter with Dolores brought me up to date on recent events. All her life, Dolores had complained about her gall bladder! Of all things!! But now, Dolores had discovered it wasn't gall bladder at all. She had a bad liver. I saw the traces of jaundice in her skin, and the tiredness in her eyes. But she was on the waiting list for a liver and luckily her name came up. The operation went successfully.

But did it go successfully? Time didn't agree. One day, Dolores stopped over to hand deliver a wedding gift to my son. She knew she was too weak to attend the wedding. I was so saddened, but I also couldn't face the truth, even as Dolores said to me, "Kathy, you know, this illness is serious. There's no guarantee on the future." Was she trying to tell me she was going to die? I really just couldn't accept that, so I just put my head down, and really didn't acknowledge her remark. I think I might have murmured "Oh, no, you're going to be fine."

Soon after, we went for what I thought would be a little walk in the neighborhood. For her, the little walk was down two houses and back. That was all she could manage. Another neighborhood friend, Najda, stopped me one day. "Kathy, can I ask a favor?" I responded, "Of course."

"Dolores is not doing well at all. Would you be willing to help out and take a shift watching her? If I can get enough people in the neighborhood to do this, we can keep her in her own home for a while longer."

"Absolutely! Of course I'll do that." What a small thing to ask, for a very, very dear lady. But I still did not accept the reality of the situation.

The next week, my husband and I went on a scheduled trip to Canada to see "Phantom of the Opera." We had a lovely time there, and came back several days later. It was a bright, cheerful, sunny day – a day in which you just gloried in being alive. After unpacking, I checked the phone message machine and there was one message that stopped me in my tracks. It was Najda. Her message? Short and simple. Dolores had died. So, while I had been enjoying the bright cheerful word of the living, the darkness of death stole in and took away my good friend.

How could that be? How could someone so young be gone from this earth. And especially Dolores!? What would her family do, her husband, her three boys.

The church, the music selections, the readings, the atmosphere, all had the understated elegance that had been so much a part of Dolores. So many friends were there, so much to reflect on. I had the occasion for a quiet talk with John, her husband.

This is the story of how Dolores died.

She had been up and around the day before. But the next day found her failing, and failing badly. A quick call to her son in Columbus brought him home immediately. Her family was there with her. By now, she was entirely jaundiced, so yellow, and her eyes were so sunken, with such a shadowed look to them. She lay there, weak, but still communicating with them. She reached her hand out to John and he held her close. He leaned in to her, and Dolores said her final words. "I gotta go now." And she breathed her last.

What did Dolores mean – "I gotta go now." Did she see something? Was someone beckoning to her? Whatever it meant, it brought such peace to John....and it ultimately left the family of five as a family of four, and a mother's earthly presence gone forever.

Once Upon A Time

Once upon a time there lived a lovely young girl. She had been blessed – she had beauty, intelligence, and a loving, giving heart. She was the oldest of three daughters born to immigrants. Keeping in line with her heritage, she had to be the responsible daughter, forever looking after her siblings. Coincidentally, her parents were named Mary and Joseph. She was the namesake child of her father, called Josephine. But Joan she became.

Although her parents only spoke broken English, and had no formal education, Joan excelled in school. She was popular, fun to be with, caring of others, and a dutiful daughter. A very dutiful daughter. Her youngest sister, Ann, had a lot of moxie – and could take care of herself. However, middle sister Mary (namesake of her mom) was as close as close could be to Joan. They did everything together. Joan made sure to take care of Mary. They went dancing together, they double dated together, they shared laughs and sobs together. They shared friends and school and sports, and enjoyed all the days of their lives together. Joan knew her place was to be the protective arm, forever keeping Mary from harm's way.

Dancing was the love of Joan's life! Her delicate feet barely touched a dance floor – she could swing and sway, and kick and shag – and she could do it all night long. She never wanted for boys to lock arms with her – she was the one they wanted to dance with. Several nights in the humid summer of '34, Joan couldn't resist.

"Mom," she asked, "Can I go out dancing tonight?"

Her mom responded, "No, you been out too much lately. I vant you stay home and geet some rest."

So, after the family was all settled in for the night, Joan swung her feet over the side of the bed, tiptoed down the hall, and flew out the door. Free, free to go dancing! She could always get a ride home once she got there. And Joan so enjoyed the freedom of dancing, dancing, dancing.

So it came one night that Joan had permission to go dancing, and to bring along Mary. Their mom gave the usual strict instructions:

"Joan, you must vatch over Mary – eet your responsibility to alvays be dere for her. Ve count on you!"

They were both just teenagers and star struck with the thought of having another opportunity to dance the night away. The Puritas Springs Ballroom was awash with glittery lights, the dance floor was packed, and the music was catchy. There was a great crowd of people dancing on the dance floor, with each couple better than the one before. Joan and Mary were a part of this merry group, all innocent kids with an enthusiasm for life, and a need for gaiety and brightness in this Depression-era time. The world was gloomy enough, but for now, on the dance floor, it was a time for the mind to be free.

The evening grew long, some kids left, and others were preparing to leave. Mary couldn't find her bag, so there was a long delay. By the time they left the ballroom, the parking lot was deserted. No quick ride home. So, off to the trolley stop for the long wait for the next trolley. The ballroom was located at the last stop on the trolley line, standing astride a deep ravine. It was a lonely, desolate spot this late at night.

While they waited, Joan and Mary laughed and exchanged excited whispers about which boys were interesting and which boys might be there again next week. As the two girls stood there and laughed, it was apparent they had just spent a great evening at this popular weekend dance hall where big band music rocked and the young people all shared the same common denominator of music and dancing.

Could luck be there for the girls? A car slowly pulled in front of them and two very nice boys called out,

"Hey, the dance is over....C'mon – we'll get you home."

Great news – now there would be no more waiting for the trolley.

Joan called to Mary, "Let's go!"

But Mary pulled back. "I didn't see them in there. They don't look familiar to me. I think we should wait for the trolley."

Joan had no concerns.

"Look, they're just kids like us. They'll have us home in no time."

So, the two young girls got in the car. For better conversation, one boy got in the back. Now there were seated as couples.

Soon Joan could see that the direction was all wrong.

Quietly, Joan said "No, no, you turned the wrong way. Go back."

And, as she glanced at the driver, it now became all too evident that this would be no pleasant ride home.

"Please pull over and just let us out here."

Still, the driver continued on. Joan glanced in the back seat at Mary. The awful reality of it pressed into her brain. She had done this. She had endangered not only herself, but her little sister. This couldn't be happening. She had read stories – bad stories – but they always happened to someone else. Now, this boy made it clear what was in store for them. Joan didn't know if Mary could hear any of this, but she couldn't take a chance.

"Please, you must understand, I can't let anything happen to my little sister."

And at that moment, she had to make a decision that would affect her all the days of her life. She offered herself up for both boys, but they must not touch Mary. Then, as the driver parked the car in the trees, he took Joan for a "walk" and when he came back, the other boy went for a "walk." It was an ugly, brutal, and cruel attack these boys committed against Joan. Her sobbing didn't stop them. They violated her innocent body and she had to withstand the pain in silence. Did they feel like big men for pinning down her small, slender frame? And forcing themselves upon her. Didn't they hear her whimpering? Didn't they feel her despair? Didn't they care? She had promised them she wouldn't fight, and she didn't. But with her body pressed down into the rough sticks and thorns of the forest floor, her pain was not only from within, but from without.

Mary couldn't understand what was going on here. Joan couldn't take the chance on alarming her, so had left the car acting as though it was a usual evening for a walk and talk in the woods. Joan knew she would have to pay dearly for her mistake. She knew that at all instances she had to protect Mary. But after what she endured that night, she was never the same person afterwards.

63

How do I know this story? When I was sixteen, the whole world was just a dancing machine to me. I loved to dance. My friends and I would "pick up" a ride on the way home. This was 1959-1960. An innocent time. My mom knew my love for dancing. One sunny summer day, out in the backyard, my mom came to talk to me.

"Kathy, you know, when I was young, I loved dancing. I was just like you. But I want to prepare you, that the world may not always be what you think it is. There is a danger out there. I want to tell you something – something very, very unpleasant. I was raped. I was raped coming home from a dance."

I couldn't think of a single thing to say to my mom. I acknowledged what she said. But I never again discussed it with her. I never probed for more information. I never again mentioned it to her – not for the next 42 years. Then, when I was 58 years old, my mom died. Now, more than ever, I realized I could never again have the opportunity to ask her about things in the past. My talking history book was gone – gone forever.

What of my Aunt Mary. She was also aged, now. But she was the only one left. The only other talking history book that could take me back to 1934 and the rape of my mother.

So I went to the nursing home to visit her with that sole purpose in mind. What would she think of me? Would she even be able to discuss this horrible incident with me? But this would be my last chance. As I sat by my aunt's bedside, I broached the subject of the rape. With a misting of her eyes, she was transported back to that dreadful time and place. And slowly, these details came to light. When my mom and Mary got back to their house that night, they had to waken their mom. Tearfully, Joan told all that had happened, all the deadly details of the night. She begged her mom's forgiveness for endangering Mary. The three of them, Mom, Joan, and Mary, had to wait and wait and wait, in silence, to be sure Joan wasn't pregnant. This was forever their hidden secret, a forever "silence", not a word to anyone. In 1934, the world would not be a forgiving place for such happenings.

Two boys committed rape. Are they disgusted with themselves? Repentant? As to be sure in life, someone is watching, waiting. We must all answer for our deeds.

One for the Road

With her angular face and Olive Oyl body, Rose never drew any attention from the boys. She put in her time at school, and upon graduation, was able to get a nice job in downtown Cleveland. She purchased a nice car, visited friends, and traveled a bit. Although her life was lonely at times, she was content.

John, on the other hand, never finished school. He was more hell bent on living on the edge. He found drinking early on, and that sealed it. He found his friend for life.

Of course, Rose and John's paths crossed. And marriage soon followed. Life was exciting for Rose. She found being part of a twosome was much more rewarding than going home alone. Yes, John's drinking worried her at times. But he was able to hold a nice job, and their finances were in order. Along came the first child, named Melinda. Melinda was a chubby baby, and grew up to keep that baby fat. She was a pretty blond baby girl, though. In short order, Trina arrived. Trina was the pixie – so elfin and slight of build – and with such enormous brown eyes! What a beauty!

But about five years into the marriage, the delicate balance began to change. John lost his job. He just lost interest – it interfered with his drinking. Rose had to go back to work. Her car was her savior. She was still able to maneuver and try to improve their circumstances. But then, John up and sold her car! He needed drinking money. Eventually, Rose just had to give up her job.

John became surly. His drinking began to take its toll. He lashed out at Rose. Loud yelling and arguing became a way of life. Soon came the agony of filling out welfare papers. Constant moving, one place worse than the previous. Tumble down neighborhoods, rough sections of town. Rose deteriorated from lack of nutritional foods. Bones jutted from her arms, her legs, from everywhere. Her face became blotchy.

The two young children knew no other way of life. Wasn't this how it was everywhere? With parents who fought, and a father who hit the mother? Wasn't drinking the norm? Weren't battle scarred, mismatched pieces of furniture and second hand dishes how every house was furnished? And oh yes, as inner city kids they were bused far away from their own neighborhood, across town, to a school that was predominately black. As they were the few white kids in class, the girls huddled together for support. They were subjected to catcalls and abuse and hateful teasing, day in and day out. It never stopped. Both children just kept their eyes straight ahead, didn't try to make friends. After all, who would be their friend? They kept to their books, and studied. They tried to close out the battles at home.

Rose loved them, but by now she was drowning in the sea of drunken rages that battered down upon her. But a mother's love is a thing to behold, and although her life had turned into a hellish nightmare on earth, she was still able to muster up her mother's courage to always protect her children from any physical abuse.

But what about the mental abuse? The emotional abuse? The financial abuse? Melinda and Trina just stayed to their books. On the rare occasions when John and Rose visited relatives, Rose could boast of her straight-A students. Yes, Melinda and Trina excelled at their schoolwork.

A close friend, Marilyn, had observed what had progressed for this family. She found it impossible to interfere, though. The one time she suggested to Rose that she just leave, Rose had replied, "Marilyn, he's threatened to harm my parents if I ever leave." And so, Rose stayed in the marriage. Marilyn ached so for Rose, to see her in a life of pain, of misery, of hopelessness.

But, Marilyn had one plan in her head. She was just biding her time. With the poverty level of this family, and the great grades the girls were getting, Marilyn felt they were a shoo-in for college. There most certainly would be grants and scholarships available for them! Marilyn just had to wait until they were sixteen and she could start putting her plans in action.

And yes, a plan was put in action, but it certainly wasn't the one Marilyn had hoped for.

When you put two little girls in a life situation of poverty, busing to a school at some far-away location, and a very dysfunctional family life, the results can be so heartbreaking. Marilyn was at home when she fielded the phone call – the phone call that told her Melinda was pregnant. Pregnant from a fellow student – a young black boy who had no intentions of marriage. Although Melinda had clung to him as someone who cared for her, he certainly had no thoughts along those lines. She was just a victory won. Marilyn had to digest this bitter news and was left to wonder how Melinda would survive now.

Soon after, Trina, too, was pregnant. Both girls had bi-racial children. John tolerated them for a time. But then, both girls were left to their own devices. John threw them out as he blubbered in his half-drunken stupor state,

"Get out of here with your black children."

Somehow, Marilyn lost track of the family. The distance was as if they were in another country. Who knows where they all live now? No mention of them, no phone calls, no one heard from them anymore. Oh, they must be around somewhere. But where? What are they doing? What are the children doing? Where are they all?

Kibo

The Facebook page popped out at me. There it was! The beautiful face, the pleading eyes. The caption read: "Won't you please take me home. My days are numbered. Two year old Shepherd mix." The information below listed Independence, and I thought 'yes', that isn't so far to go to fetch this dog and for sure this is the dog I want. I had been thinking for months of taking on the responsibility of dog ownership. I knew it couldn't be a passing fancy. I had to be a forever home. And now I was ready.

I responded to the posting immediately. Yes, I will take this dog. In the next few days it became quite complicated, and I couldn't understand why. One of my first instructions was to get a note of approval from my vet with my history of pet ownership. But the next instruction was rather far-fetched I felt. I received an email that I would have to pass a home inspection. I was not adopting a child. I couldn't fathom this mandate.

Finally, I approached one of the Realtors in my office who was a volunteer at a local rescue group. He proved marvelous. He consulted with the head of his local rescue group and was able to cut through all this red tape and get the necessary approvals for me. It was only at this point that I realized why such close scrutiny. The ad had stated Independence, which I assumed was Independence, Ohio. Never did I think of Independence,

Missouri! Therefore, the reason for all these mandates. The shelter frowned on an out-of-state adoption. Unfortunately, some people take a pound dog for nefarious reasons. This shelter wanted reassurances that I would be a legitimate owner. I was never one to back off from a situation, and I was so committed at this point that nothing could stop me. I would gladly drive to Missouri. Two wonderful volunteers offered to get the dog through St. Louis so I wouldn't have to deal with lots of traffic, and meet me in a highway restaurant parking lot for the handoff. This was ideal for me.

One of my wonderful friends, Jane, offered to make this memorable trip with me. We set off after work on our 'girl trip' and drove through Ohio and Indiana, stopping just short of Missouri. We wanted to be fresh from our journey, so we got a room for the night, and in the morning, continued on. Everything went as planned, and we met these two lovely volunteers along with my new four-legged friend. The exchange happened so quickly, and before I knew it, Jane and I were back on the road for the return trip. Doggie was so docile, just sleeping in the back seat. He slept for almost the entire trip home. Unknown to me he had recently had the surgery to "fix" him. When I look back at this, I wonder why the time and expense of "fixing" him, if he was labeled for euthanasia.

The next morning, I finally had a chance to review all the documents and papers that I received in the handoff. My doggie's name originally had been Lucky Boy. When he ended up at the high-kill shelter, his name was changed to Poor Lucky Boy. I didn't have the heart to come up with yet another name, so I tried to use part of his name already in existence. I looked at Lucky Boy, shortened it to Keyboy, but that proved difficult to pronounce. Keyboy became Kibo, and I was happy with this new name.

I had a new best buddy. From reading the paperwork, I learned that Kibo was first given to the first owner, a young man. However, this fellow seemingly ran into financial problems and couldn't afford to feed him. He turned the dog over to a friend. The friend was able to keep the dog for a short time, but in view of the fact that he already had two dogs, he was ready to hand off Kibo. He took Kibo to the local shelter, and there my poor baby languished.

So in essence, Kibo in his short 2-year life span, had now lived at 5 different places. Place of birth, young man, young man's friend, shelter, and now my house. I took the term 'forever home' to heart, and knew there would be no more homes for Kibo. He was here to stay. He was now my buddy and I had a constant companion. My home would be his last handoff, his last home.

We did everything together. First, I had to get some decent training for him and I found a wonderful trainer. We worked on 'heel', 'sit', 'stay' and other basic commands. But the best of all was when I learned that Kibo would run alongside my bicycle. I attached a leash to the side of my bike, kept it very short, and Kibo learned to keep stride all the way. I had a speedometer on my bike, and we always reached 15 mph. Quite scary. I didn't even have to pedal. Kibo loved stretching his legs to the fullest. It was quite a sight in the neighborhood. Woman and dog, tearing down the side streets at a full run. Our round-trip came in at one mile.

Then, there were the walks in the woods. I had installed an Invisible Fence in the yard, and the leash that came with that program was over fourteen feet long. Kibo was able to walk to the side of the trail and appreciate all the smells and scents left by other dogs.

The calendar pages of my life flipped like Autumn leaves in the wind. In the next three years we formed a solid bond. If I read in the Living Room, Kibo was by my side. Family Room for television, Kibo right by my side. Kitchen for a meal, there was my Kibo. Sleep time, Kibo right by me. My son once remarked, "Mom, no matter what room you go into, Kibo goes with you".

Unfortunately, life sneaks up on us and upsets the best laid plans of man.

I had Kibo for five years. I lost Kibo for no reason. I lost Kibo because of greediness.

I was in the backyard doing what I love most, yardwork. I heard a slight commotion in the front yard. I came along the side of my house to see what was happening. Across the street were three girls, and one was crying. As I came down my driveway, my next door neighbor called out, "Kathy, I was right here and saw it. Your dog was on his property." I rushed across the street. Apparently these three girls had been hired by a local pizza store to deliver flyers in the area. As they came up my walkway and approached my front door, Kibo rushed to chase them away.

Kibo had been watching the neighborhood, and when he saw three girls, laughing and talking, come up to the house, he tried to scare them off. Unfortunately, as the teenagers turned to get away, Kibo jumped up and scratched one of the teenagers on her back. Whew, nothing serious. An abrasion like you might experience from falling off your bike, scraping yourself. My neighbor approached. We all checked the injury yet again, and remarked at the scratch marks. After asking the girls if we could do anything for them, some more crying gushed forth, and finally they just left.

Later in the day the police department called me and asked me to come in and give a statement regarding this incident. I went right up. From what I could gather from the young officer, the girl's father had been there and had been very insistent that the police do something about my dog. But the officer ascertained that my dog had been on his own property and therefore was not a 'dog at large'. Therefore, they would do nothing in the matter. He said the father was quite verbal and quite insistent, demanding the police do something about the matter. The officer repeated again to the father that the dog was on its own property, therefore, no action would be taken. I listened to all this and filed it away in my memory. Finally, I completed the papers, thanked the officer, and left.

Several days later I received notice from the County to quarantine my dog for one week. No problem. Except, on the notification, I crossed out the part that said 'dog bite' and inserted the word 'scratch'. Then I mailed it in.

Life continued on, and Kibo and I had so many great times. I just had to say the words 'car ride' or 'walk' or 'bike' and Kibo was raring to go. Month after month went by and life was good.

About ten months after the incident, I received a letter from an attorney regarding the matter. The gist of the letter was that the attorney only wanted the name of my insurance company. I could not believe it! What a ripoff. Sure, someone just wanted money and a quickie payment from my insurance company for some nonsensical and supposed injury. I was incensed. There had been no real injury. Yes, a scratch. This was ten months later! What was going on. I refused to be intimidated. I ignored the letter. The following month I received the same identical letter again – it had been photocopied. Across the front of the letter, written in ink, were the words "second

75

request." I ignored this, too. I would gladly go toe to toe with this attorney if he kept this up.

Well, the third month, yet another letter arrived stating further legal action. At this point, I called my insurance company to say that I would just as soon deal with this myself. The response? No, No, you can't do that. That's what we're here for. Use us. That's why you have insurance. So I gave all the necessary details.

More months went by. Now, almost another year had passed. My beautiful Kibo had now been with me for five years. We had a bond, a love for each other. We were one and the same on our hikes through the many nearby wooded trails. Kibo had been loaded into the car for the five-hour trek to visit my son down near Cincinnati so many times that he knew the way. He would always feel it when we got within a mile of the house. On the return trip, same thing. Kibo always knew when we were getting close to our home.

During this period of time, I followed up once with the insurance company. The very nice lady on the 'case' said they had just received the picture of the injury. After all those many months, the attorney finally sent one that was taken at the time of the incident. She remarked,

"Goodness, it looks like a scratch."

I responded, "Yes, it's a scratch."

A few days later I received a letter stating the case was being transferred to another contact person. I kept the name on file for my reference.

In the Springtime of the next year I was enjoying a lovely walk with Kibo along a gorgeous stream. I took pictures to post to Facebook. There was Kibo, gazing down at the creek. Yet again, Kibo obeying my command to 'sit' on the trail so I could take another picture. If you ever want to feel 'one with nature' just walk along an isolated wooded path with your dog. Time to contemplate, to renew yourself, to heal your soul from all of life's ravages.

The very next day, a beautiful Spring day, I retrieved my mail and noticed an envelope from my insurance company. I deduced immediately it was probably about this old matter with my dog. Good, hopefully this would be behind me now. But no. Inside was a cancellation on my insurance policy.

I rattled through my file drawer and came up with that name of my most recent contact person. Of course, I called immediately. The lady was so nice. I told her about the cancellation notice and eventually the discussion turned to my dog. Kibo, as usual, was at my feet.....always with me. I looked down at him as I was talking. Soon, the conversation turned to the reasons for termination of my policy. Of course, she said it was due to this 'unsettled' case. My goodness, almost two years had gone by. I couldn't believe it hadn't been settled.

Finally, I asked, "Well, how much **is** the settlement?"

She responded "$14,000, but we are still in negotiation. The people do not want us to pay the money yet until their daughter turns 18."

Then she said words to the effect it would be easier for the family to transfer the money once the daughter turned of age, which would be in July. I almost fell out of my chair. What in the name of heaven was going on?

I said, "But it was a scratch. My dog was on his own property."

Then she went on to inform me of Ohio laws, and I was dumfounded. In layman terms, this is the information I received. A dog owner can post to his heart's content – post signs that say 'beware of dog', 'keep away', but they actually have no clout, no protection whatsoever, for the dog owner. The dog owner would have to prove that someone coming on their property was literally killing their dog in order for a court to side with the dog owner if an injury occurred. Not only that, but the payoff is higher for a girl over a boy. Supposedly because 'looks', or a scar, matter more to a girl than a boy. But why so much money. Oh, no, I was assured, this was par for the course. My head was spinning with all that was being said.

This was ridiculous. How many times had dogs jumped up on me. How many times had a dog 'nipped' in play, or some other such action. All the time!

We went on to talk about the cancellation, and just as we were winding up the conversation, she threw this out at me.

"Do you still have the dog?"

I replied, "Yes."

"Then I feel obligated to tell you that now, since this is on record, you can be considered 'harboring a dangerous animal." You will no longer be able to have this dog insured, and if any occurrence happened in the future, you would now be the one paying $14,000 or even more."

I responded, "But it was just a scratch."

She replied, "Scratch, bite, it makes no difference. She was injured."

I sat there in a stupor. This couldn't be. I looked down at my beautiful Kibo and he was looking at me with such trust in his eyes. He was waiting for any indication that we would take off on a walk, or another adventure in life. But I sat there frozen in place.

I remember hanging up the phone, and sitting, and sitting, and sitting. Thoughts were racing through my mind. What could I do? What should I do? What can I do? I certainly can't give my dog to someone else and put the burden on them. I couldn't lie and give my dog away, and not mention this most horrific stigma. I could not take my dog to a rescue site. I could not withhold this information.

So I sat there in complete and utter anguish. Inside deep sobs engulfed me. Did I have to do the very unthinkable act? OH NO! This can't be happening. No, No, No. My head couldn't get around this horrible situation. Just yesterday, Kibo and I had been in the woods, at peace with nature. I looked down at my beloved dog, and felt the cruelty of life crushing in on me. The only thing pounding in my head was I had no choice but to end his life. My body literally collapsed. I knelt down beside Kibo and hugged him, and kissed him, and pressed him to me. I cried in his fur. Would there be no release. Please, please, let this be over. No, I couldn't allow myself the luxury to think. I had to do the unthinkable. Oh my God, I wasn't capable of what was required of me. What cruel, cruel system would demand this of me. I had to become a robot. I had to do things robotically. Call on the phone. Call the vet. Tell them what was happening. Tell them I needed an appointment then and now. I couldn't deal with this torment another minute. It was 11:00 in the morning. The vet said they could take me at 3:00.

I sat in a chair, with Kibo in front of me. He looked at me, not understanding the sobs shaking

my body. He leaned into me, trying to console me.
I did not move for the next four hours. For four
hours I sat there, looking into my Kibo's trusting
eyes, knowing his life would be over in just a few
hours. I stayed right in that chair. I did not feel I
had a right to move. I had no right to do what was
planned. I had lost my soul, my heart, my being.

The fated hour arrived, and Kibo jumped up
eagerly, willingly, as I led him to his death. Oh no.
Even today, I cannot release myself from the pain.
Kibo was so excited to see me reach for his leash.
Aha! Another adventure. Another fun time with
my owner. He gladly jumped in the back seat for
this most wonderful excursion. The drive was
short. Everyone in the vet office must have
known about this fated visit. I was taken
immediately. They led Kibo over to a scale.

I said, "No. You don't need to weigh him."

They said, "Yes, we do."

And then it hit me. They needed to know
his weight in order to prepare a correct dosage.

Kibo was so interested in everything. He
went back and forth, taking in all the smells and
sounds and activity going on in the waiting room.
Kibo loved life. At 67#, his energy level had
always been off the wall.

They led us back to a room I had never been
in before. It was a large room. An empty room,

save for some cabinets along the perimeter, and a lonely blanket placed right in the middle of the room. It was white, stark, and forbidding. Kibo, of course, went off to explore every nook and cranny in the room. I watched as if from a long way off. My mind just wasn't functioning. From far away I heard the vet say she was going to take my beloved pet with her to administer some kind of shot to make him drowsy.

After a short time, she returned. Kibo was still alert. Once again I was with my most precious, sweet baby. The vet left the room. I sat on the blanket and watched as Kibo sniffed around the room. He circled and circled in his curiosity. I had to go off to another place in my mind, or I would have collapsed. Then, just like that, Kibo came around the room, neared the blanket, and his leg collapsed. He fell on the blanket, right by me. I cannot describe the utter and complete anguish enveloping every fiber of my being. My dog loved me. My dog trusted me. And now, here, I led him to his destruction. No, inwardly I fought this over and over. But he lay there. Just about then, the vet re-entered the room.

"Now, I will be administering the final shot. You can stay right there by him. You may notice at the very end he will let out some final exhaling of his lungs. There might be about three to five of these."

I did not turn my head to watch her. I held on tightly to his head, keeping my face muffled in his fur. His eyes were closed. He was in a deep sleep. I kept repeating over and over and over again, "Kibo, I love you. You're my good baby. I love you. You're such a good baby. I love you forever, and ever."

And soon, of course, came the last involuntary gulps. No, NO! Kibo could NOT be there, now, on the blanket, dead. Dead. I slumped down next to him. I just wanted to be with him, forever and forever. Oh dear Lord, how permanent death is. There is no going back. My baby is gone…gone from me forever. The world is a horrible, horrible place.

Thankfully, the vet left the room, and I sat in silence for a long, long time. I just kept petting my beautiful Kibo and saying over and over again, "I'm so sorry, so sorry, please forgive me."

Eventually three people were in the room with me. The vet asked me to get my car, and the two assistants said they would then load my baby's body into my car. This was done.

I had made the decision I would not involve my family, my friends, in the terrible ordeal of the past four hours. I did not want to spread my heartbreak on anyone else. I knew this was something I had to do by myself. But on the drive home, I phoned a dear friend and asked her to come to my house. Briefly, I tried to explain what had been done. She was there when I pulled onto the drive. I opened to hatchback of my car, and it was surreal. My angel just looked like he was sleeping, right there in the back of the car. Not a hair was touched, not a mark on him.

I had a beautiful spot, right in the front flowerbed, where I knew Kibo loved to sunbathe when he was out in the yard. This, then, would be his final resting place. I dug and dug, but I knew I couldn't dig far enough on my own. I called my son-in-law, and lucky for me he was available. He came right over. The final moments were facing me now. He gently lifted my Kibo out of the car and managed to get him to the burial site. I had lined the hole with soft blankets and Kibo's favorite ball. Everything was a blur. Surreal.

Then, my son-in-law slowly lowered my precious Kibo down, down, down. I looked at my lovely dog. He trusted me in all things and I made the final betrayal. How, oh how, could this have happened. I asked everyone to leave. I went into the house. Alone, so alone without my Kibo.

I now have my memories. I have my pictures. I have my videos. I have a lovely headstone up front. It simply says, 'Kibo, Always In My Heart."

Some may think I acted too quickly. That there might have been another solution. But ultimately I could not pass on to someone else the stigma that had been placed on my beloved Kibo. What recourse is there, once the verdict comes down, that you are now "harboring a dangerous animal." Yes, life can be unfair.

Oh yes. Some family is so happy they have $14,000. And I have my memories.

Mr. Jamison

I was elated! My hard work was paying off!! Mr. Jamison from down the street had just called and asked me to stop over to talk about listing his house. Double luck for me! One, it was always a good thing to get a listing in your own neighborhood. But also, it looked like all my personal promotional ideas were paying off.

I prepared all my materials and set off for our evening appointment. Mr. Jamison was most definitely a kind, considerate gentleman. Although he lived only eight doors down from me, I never really talked to him or got to know him as more than just 'the neighbor down the street'.

As we walked through the house, he described each room and the improvements that had been made. Actually, the house was dark and a little dreary for my taste. The walls echoed 60's decorating, and the front yard was a bit overgrown.

Mr. Jamison said, "Thank you for taking the time to come over. It's been rather lonely since my wife passed away. I appreciate your honest pricing opinion and I'll be in touch with you soon."

I really wanted the listing but I thought perhaps he wasn't pleased with my price opinion. I knew he was going to talk to another Realtor®, so I took a wait and see attitude. He wasn't the type of gentleman you wanted to hit with a "hard sell" approach. His tired eyes and his slouched over posture indicated a life of hard work and worry and sleepless nights. Well, I thought, just typical of what I would expect in an old man.

Later that week, I got the call I had been hoping for.

Mr. Jamison said, "Hello Kathy. I'm up here at the Finger Lakes. I've been doing a lot of thinking, mulling over my options, and have decided to go ahead with you. Problem is, though, that I don't intend to come back to the area any time soon. Is there any way you can bring the paperwork up to me?"

Big problem? Geeeez – that would be one **long** drive! Lonely, too. But then, my daughter was home from college and maybe I could convince her to take the long drive with me. We could use the opportunity for some mother-daughter bonding! And my wonderful daughter agreed to take the drive with me.

Soon after pulling into the camping grounds, we located his trailer hookup. Mr. Jamison stood from his lawn chair.

I called out, "Mr. Jamison, Hi!" and introduced him to my daughter Linda. "Wow, this sure is a scenic place – looks nice and sleepy and restful. I see you have your fishing gear out."

Mr. Jamison was definitely in his element. I could just imagine, after losing his soulmate, his lovely wife, that this would be just the place to heal your mind, your soul, your heart.   The stately trees and shimmering lake lent a sense of peace to the overall atmosphere. The sun glowed as it sent its warming rays over us and the whispering laps of the water gave an essence of peace and tranquility. It was one of those moments you hold in your mind – all was so right with the world here.

Well, Mr. Jamison had even more to share with us. He had planned a small trip to the nearest town to treat us to lunch. How very proud he was as we piled into his little truck and took off for his favorite eatery. Typical small-time America, that was my feeling during this entire adventure. We had a tasty meal and Mr. Jamison had so much fun showing us the 'sights'. I felt him really coming alive with feelings and a certain excitement about life again. He was a grand old fellow that afternoon.

Later, we filled out all our necessary paperwork and gradually said our goodbyes. I assured Mr. Jamison that I would look after the house, and find a buyer as quickly as I could. Soon after, an acceptable offer came in and we closed on the house. About this time, I met again with Mr. Jamison for a final accounting. And Mr. Jamison told me his story.

His beloved wife had emphysema. And of course, the disease only worsened with time.

Mr. Jamison said, "At first, she could still get around and go places and share everyday activities with me. Gradually, she spent less time doing things, and more time sitting. Even this deteriorated until she finally spent more time in bed than anywhere else. On those few occasions when she had to travel, she would run out of breath just walking from the kitchen door to the enclosed garage and car. I never slept through a night. I went to her many times to check on her, to reassure her that I was there. Day after day, month after month. This disease does its dirty business over a long period of time. I could only sit back and watch my faithful partner become a shell of her former self. Kathy, let me tell you about the final night. She was sleeping. I was tossing and turning, listening to her oxygen concentrator – taking the air into her machine, filtering it, and sending it back as pure oxygen. I heard her call to me and I went to her side. She looked at me with her tired, gentle eyes. I looked down at her. What could I read in her beloved face. Was she looking at me with the wish to live? Or the wish to die? And this is what she whispered to me. "Andrew, call 911. I'm dying. And I did, and she did.

Now the house that flourished with our family, our five kids running, jumping, having friends over, Sunday meals, holiday visits – that's all over for me now. I don't want the house – the memories are in my mind. I don't need a house to tell me about the love we had, and the dreams we shared. She breathed her last. And now, I'll sit in my chair, by the lake, with my sun drenched battered hat, and I'll breathe in the fresh air in a way she never could. And I'll wish she could be here with me, breathing in the sweet soft air."

As he walked away, I knew I would never see him again, or even hear from him. Our paths had touched briefly, for just that slightest bit of time.

As I sit here today, I can picture him in my mind, relaxing in his lawn chair with his battered old hat, fishing pole in hand, with a faraway look in his eyes, just remembering.

Linda

There's a lonely stretch of road in Avon Lake, Ohio that runs parallel to a main railroad track for approximately two miles. You can go out there and measure it on your odometer – just two miles from one end to the other. There are only four homes scattered along the way and it is a favorite shortcut for many motorists.

One December, whether due to my melancholy mood or my desire to bring a special moment into Christmas, I followed through on an idea that had been in my mind for years, many years. I had always noticed the slight pine trees on the embankment by these tracks, some large, some very small, but only just a few. That past summer, crews had come along and pulled out some old railroad ties, replacing them with new ones. In doing so, they just threw the old ties down the embankment to be picked up later. As they fell, some knocked over the pine trees, leaving them bent over along the way. I found this very sad, that a once proud tree was now bent due to man's haste.

There was one teeny little tree, however, just small enough to decorate for Christmas. That's what I set out to do. I would take just enough time to park my car along the edge of the road, leap the ditch, and climb the slight embankment to the halfway point, where the tree was firmly planted. Then I could wrap a garland around the tree and give it some Christmas cheer. I know I was hoping that as people passed this lonely sight and saw my tiny tree just simply wrapped in garland that they, too, would feel a magical warmth during the Christmas season.

So, just before Christmas, I put my plan into action. I bought a new, fresh garland and drove over to the little tree. I leaped over the ditch and started my decorating. Because of the incline, I kept losing my footing as I went round and round the tree, but I finally finished.

Several days later, my 25-year-old daughter, Linda, and I were going Christmas shopping and had to pass this very spot. I was really eager to hear what Linda would say about this strange little sight.

She called out, "Mom, look what someone's done. That tree over there is sparkling with a little garland."

Of course, I couldn't keep my secret. Linda and I have always shared so much. She has always been what a mother would like in a daughter. Her very petite frame, 4'11" and 95 pounds encompasses a warm and kind person. She is lovely to look at, but better yet, she is lovely to know. She demonstrates this over and over in her role as a first grade teacher.

"Linda, I decorated that tree. And I'm really hoping that as other people pass by, they too, might add to what I've done. Wouldn't it be great if others added an ornament or two and that by

Christmas Eve, the tree was all decorated in a glorious splendor." We both agreed that would be really special.

Just a couple of days later, we again went shopping and of course passed 'my' tree again. But this time I was the one in absolute awe. I couldn't believe it. Lo and behold, beautiful red ornaments now hung proudly in the little Christmas tree. Oh, someone else had believed as I had believed. There was a special feeling at Christmas, not just shopping for material things, but for a shared moment – a moment that represented a special warmth for Christmas. This was a simple beauty not to be compared to fighting the crowds in the stores and beating someone for the closest parking space.

In the last days before Christmas, I had many occasions to travel this road, sometimes alone, but many times with my daughter. Our last trip was on December 24th, late in the afternoon. Sure as anything, there was the tree, all aglitter with its garland and ornaments.

As we passed by, Linda said, "Mom, there's something I've been wanting to tell you. You know how much you wanted to feel that people would join you in decorating that lonely little tree on this deserted road? Well, I felt that way, too. And I didn't want you to be out there all alone with your idea not taking root. So, mom, I was the one who added my decorations to your decorations."

I should have known. I should have known that my Linda would have the insight to be the sole contributor to my tree, to make me feel that people **did** care. That there was a special significance and splendor to a tiny tree by a dirty railroad track, adorned so simply by two individuals, and one not knowing who the other was. And here, it was my own daughter.

Christmas came and went and I was preparing to leave the house to gather up the ornaments from the tree. I didn't feel it was right to leave the decorating up and abandon the little tree. It was a bitter cold January day, with a wind chill factor of at least 10 below zero. Linda volunteered to go with me, thereby allowing me to just park the car with the motor running, while she jumped out and gathered up all the decorations. In our haste, Linda forgot her gloves but I never realized it until I looked out the window and saw her frozen little fingers, all red and cold as ice, as she tried to remove the ornaments. They were sticking to the pine needles, as was the garland. Her fingers looked numb from the cold as she tried to hold her coat as an apron so she could stack the decorations in there. It took much longer than I thought it would take. When Linda finally slid down the embankment and unloaded the decorations into the back seat, I could see she was freezing. When she scrambled into the front seat with me, I closed my gloved hands around hers and held it up to the blower vent to get instant warmth into her fingers. I felt so sorry for her – she was so helpful and never complained.

Every time I look back on the events of that Christmas, and of 'my' little tree, I feel a 'oneness' with Linda. I don't remember the gifts I received that Christmas, or the ones I gave. What I do remember, however, is that moment in time – a closeness shared. It was the best gift of all, that precious memory. It would never break, tarnish, go out of style, or get lost. It would only grow more special as the years went on.

Just recently, Linda got married, and she will now forge her way in life. Along the way, I wonder if she, too, will always remember the Christmas she gave me the best present of all, this precious memory which is truly the most lasting gift of all.

Cracked, but not Broken

When I was a little girl, I truly believed that everyone grew up and found happiness. Even when my sister cracked up in the late 50's, I still believed that everything was fine with the world. So what if she laughed incessantly in our cramped, little bedroom every night. So what if she said Thor "made her do it" when she flew off the handle. So what if she was losing her mind. My family was reassuring. We would all be fine. When we sat in church on Sundays our whole family lined up in a pew – mom, dad, my two sisters, my brother and me. Patricia would start her giggling and laughing but I wasn't alarmed. My parents weren't alarmed, so I wasn't. This went on for months.

Finally one day, Patricia was gone. I knew my parents had finally found an opening for her at the Metropolitan Hospital's Mental Ward. Mom was now nine months pregnant, and she was relieved that Patricia was now getting needed care. She could finally allow herself to go ahead and have the new baby. This newest baby would make the fifth child.

Soon, mom got home from the hospital with our new little sister, Christine. Time passed, month after month. Then, Patricia got to come home for weekends with us. I knew she had some kind of "shock" treatment. But Patricia also told me that she was able to "fool" the doctors. She didn't tell them everything. Eventually, Patricia was released to live at home once again with all of us, supposedly cured. Looking back, I guess in the 50's, mental health was still an overlooked condition, and no in-depth treatment was readily available.

So what has happened between 1958 and 2017? Patricia never did leave home. She lived with my parents all her life. There were no group homes back then. There were no "planned activities" or "socials" for someone with mental issues. She spent the rest of her years struggling, able to carry on a conversation, but not a lot of substance. Smart enough to know what she was missing but not smart enough to achieve it. It has not escaped her that she never married, never had children, never had a home of her own. She sees her siblings, all with families, all grandparents now. She knows that she missed out.

My parents are now gone. Patricia is now in a senior apartment complex, all alone. We all visit her, and include her in holiday events, and dining out on weekends. But the fact is, she never grew up to find happiness - the happiness I thought everyone experienced in their lifetimes. Her years have raced by. She is now in her 70's. She has great capacity in some areas. She can be most thoughtful sometimes. And other times, she can show the frustration of a ten-year old. At one time we tried to explore more opportunities for her, but ultimately, it was too late.

Now I'm old enough to know that no one guarantees us happiness. Some of us achieve it, others never do. Or, some have brief glimpses of it, and some never even have that. Happiness, oh happiness, wherefore art thou, oh happiness.

Eating Alone

Even though the old woman let us in the door, I was not really aware of her until I went through her kitchen. I had been explaining all the nice amenities of the home to my customers, and we had been taking our time as we passed through each room. When we arrived in the kitchen, however, the old woman was seated there at a tiny table. She had a small meal in front of her, and I couldn't get over how very frail and vulnerable she looked.

As my customers looked into every nook and cranny in the room, and then continued on out into the Living Room, I stopped for a moment to address this older person. I don't remember what kind of small talk I tried to make, but I will always remember her final response. I must have asked something about why she was selling her house and she said she was going to a home. Her husband had just died.

As she sat there, dabbing away at the bits of food, she looked up at me with haunting eyes. She asked, "Do you know what the loneliest thing in the world is?" As I stood there thinking about her question, she answered it herself, in low tones, with the simple words, "Eating Alone." I couldn't help but choke back a quiet sob in the back of my throat.

The Wig

It was stark, freezing weather in a typical cold, blasting Northeast Ohio winter. My customer and I had agreed to meet in front of the house. Boy! Was it hard to get this appointment. The owner had told me over the phone that she was sick, but I was determined to get the showing in that evening, so I persisted.

I told her, "Yes, I've been sick, too. Lots of colds and flu going around."

And I did convince her to allow the showing.

After entering the home, my customers meandered through the rooms, while I hung back to reassure the owner that we wouldn't be there long. Again, she mentioned that she was very sick. And again I told her I understood. I was a bit under the weather also. Flu was attacking everyone.

"No," she said. "I'm really sick."

And at that moment she proceeded to tug at her hair and as I watched, unbelievably, she removed a wig. She was totally bald.

"Yes," she said. "I have cancer – I'm going through chemotherapy. As I said, I'm very sick."

My small case of the flu paled in comparison to what this woman was going through. My heart went out to her.

I see a lot of situations in my real estate career. Sometimes people are selling their home for a happy reason. Other times, they are selling because of a tragedy, or hard times, or health issues. We never know what circumstances can force their way into our lives. What will the future hold? Only time will tell.

The Tenants

Realtor® Patty listed a nice split-level home in a great area. This was sure to be money in the bank. She couldn't see this property languishing on the market – it was priced right, and the seller was motivated. There was one catch, however. The home had tenants. As Realtors® know, tenants have no motivation at all for the home they live in to sell out from under them. They have no idea if the new owners will hold the rent amount, or have them leave when the lease is up. So, since the tenant is up in the air about whether he will have to move or not, he surely isn't going to be the most cooperative person in the world when it comes to "showings."

Patty was about to learn this the hard way. She did manage to squeeze in a couple of showings, but no buyer yet. So, next, she scheduled a nice Sunday open house. She gingerly called the tenants to be sure the house would be ready for the open house, and to remind them to leave the premises between 2:00 and 5:00, the hours of her open house.

Sunday came, and she arrived promptly. The tenants let her in, and she set up about arranging her materials on the kitchen counter. She was rather dismayed at the condition of the rooms, all messy and certainly not in good order at all. And the tenants were lying around in their bedclothes! Patty figured she could straighten up some of the rooms after the tenants left. But the tenants didn't leave!

While she was setting up, they were setting up, too. That is, setting up in front of the TV set for the Sunday football game. And not just that, but they also set up their six-packs! Some of their friends showed up to join in this nightmare Patty was having. Now, Patty is a downright determined person and no one is going to scare her off. So, she just proceeded with the open house. Sure enough, some home-seekers arrived to check out the property. Patty tried to ignore walking around everyone's bare-feet sticking out everywhere in the living room to show the customers around.

After the third or fourth customer came to the open house, the tenants got rather surly. Now, in addition to their sloppy bedclothes, their six-packs, their rowdy friends, their loud burping and farting, they started to shout out things to each customer who came through. "The roof leaks!" "The basement has water!" "There's bad plumbing in the bathroom!" This whole brouhaha was ridiculous. Why, oh why, Patty thought, didn't I just leave from the get-go!!

Finally, the magic hour of 5:00 arrived and Patty bolted for the door, sobbing when she got to her car. A week later, she sold the home! So much for the uncooperative tenants! But it's a day of infamy that Patty will not soon forget! The Terrible Tenants!!

The Mystery of The Statue

Virginia Coyle was the neighbor everyone would like to have. Friendly, but not overpowering. Helpful, but not obnoxious. She raised her nine children right in that house across the street from me.

Well, Virginia did her job well. Raised all nine of those kids, but now she was alone. Her husband died, the kids all moved to other states, and even her cat was gone. However, even more seriously, her mind was going. Whether it was the beginnings of Alzheimer's or dementia, or just plain forgetfulness, who knew in these early stages. But the writing was on the wall. She couldn't stay in her house, alone, any longer.

Son Mike signed the necessary paperwork with me to put her house on the market. It was tough for me to see that house, right across the street, with my name and real estate company phone number on the sign, and know that soon I would have new neighbors.

The house was basically original in all its components, and a little old fashioned in its decorating. It didn't sell right away. Eventually, Mike had to actually take a leave of absence from his job in New York, and come to stay with Virginia. Each day he would see me across the street and walk over to ask if there were any potential buyers yet. And each day, I would have to say "no".

Well, there is a patron saint for "selling houses", or so they say. And that patron saint is St. Joseph! I had heard all the stories already, from other Realtors, about houses they had listed that just didn't sell. They would tell their customers to bury a St. Joseph statue in the yard, and that would bring a sale. In all these stories that were told to me, a buyer **did** show up soon after! I'd also heard that you had to bury St. Joseph face down to the east, or face up to the west, or upside down to the south. I heard so many different variations that it all became a garbled message. But, as a last resort, I told Mike to get a St. Joseph statue and bury it in the yard.

I was amazed! Not one week later, we found a buyer. All went well. The transaction went smoothly and closed on time. That evening, my husband and I left the house to go out to dinner. As we passed by Mrs. Coyle's house, I saw Mike in the side yard, with a gaping hole that must have been at least 2 feet deep and 3 feet in diameter. We slowed down the car and stopped to ask what he was doing. Well, he had been digging for quite a while – to no avail. He was trying to recover the St. Joseph statue.

He said, "Kathy, this is exactly where I buried it. But it's not here!" You know, he never did find that statue.

Mrs. Coyle is long gone. What happened to her? I don't know. And the statue? To this day, I wonder, where did it go?

At the Curb

I knew Mrs. Patrick was a tough wiry bird from the moment I first laid eyes on her. She certainly didn't mince words, and I'm sure she earned that right at 83 years of age. I had called on many "For Sale By Owners" and could never predict the reception I would get.

When I pulled into her drive, I noted another car in the driveway, and a young man just exiting the house. I sensed instantly that it was another Realtor. But, I wasn't about to back off. So, I merely said I would be glad to move my car for him. His reaction was like a deer in the headlights. He certainly didn't want to leave and give me a shot at listing the house. But he had no alternative. Now, I had just precious moments to ingratiate myself to Mrs. Patrick, and convince her I was the Realtor to work with. Lucky for me, Mrs. Patrick believed in advertising, and just that week I had run a large full-page ad of all the homes I had for sale. This impressed her so much, and that decided it for her. She agreed to list the house with me.

In the next few weeks, I visited Mrs. Patrick several times. One beautiful fall day, I found her by the side of the house, up on a ladder! She was cleaning the gutters! And to top it off, Mrs. Patrick had great legs! Wow! I should be so lucky at 83. I also found out that she was an old, retired schoolteacher, long ago divorced. She had two sons who lived out of state – one in New York, and one in California. And she certainly had no use for men. She literally spat the word at me.

"Men, no use for 'em." She said

I always called her Mrs. Patrick – no first name comraderie with this one!

Meanwhile, her little home wasn't the greatest house. It was a summer cottage converted to house status. But, it did have one outstanding quality, the beautiful wooded lot. Eventually, an agent showing the house wrote a contract for their customer – a young, single girl buying her first house. Written in the contract was her request for a house inspection. OK, not a problem.

I arrived at the house to find the home inspector already examining way down under the house. There was no basement, no crawl space with access from the house. The only way under the house was from the outside. Eventually, he emerged, full of spider webs, dirt, grime and whatnot. I was sure no one had been down there for years. For some reason, he wouldn't let Mrs. Patrick or me follow him on the rest of the inspection. When it was over, I asked him why we couldn't have followed along.

He whispered, "The foundation is crumbling."

Whoops….now I had a major problem. I waited a day or two until the buyer had reviewed the results of the home inspection. I was anxious to see how she would accept this news. Mrs. Patrick had already told me she would not, in any way, shape, or form, participate in any money repairs that the house might need. Well, of course, the buyer came back requesting that Mrs. Patrick arrange for the repairs of the 'crumbling foundation.'

Now I was faced with the task I dreaded, going to Mrs. Patrick. After giving her the results of the inspection, and the buyer's request, Mrs. Patrick just sat there, and sat there, and sat there.

Finally she said, "Kathy, and just what will happen if the repair isn't made?"

I had to say, "Mrs. Patrick, it will only get worse, and eventually it will affect the main floor, too."

So again, she mulled this over for the longest time, and finally responded with her words of wisdom.

"Kathy, this house is in Avon Lake, and you know how values are increasing every day! Crumbling foundation or not, it will only appreciate."

And that was that. I figured this deal was as dead as can be. But surprise of surprises! The buyer wanted the house so badly, she accepted it, with no repair!

Before moving day, Mrs. Patrick had a garage sale. I stopped over early in the evening only to find her very, very upset. She held out her hand, with a wad of bills clenched tightly in her fist.

"Kathy, I only made $300."

I was pleased. I thought she had done really well, considering her things were very old. But, it turned out Mrs. Patrick was extremely disappointed! She felt she should have earned much more. But even more alarming to me was when I spotted tears in her eyes. She wanted to continue on with what she was saying, but there was a pregnant pause, and.....nothing. I just stood there, not knowing what to do. I was so stunned to see her eyes brimming with tears.

Finally, she said, "Kathy, I want to speak, but I can't think of what I'm saying. I think.....I think I had a stroke earlier."

I was devastated. But in my youth, I didn't know that much about those matters. I urged her to go to the hospital, but she assured me she would be okay. I couldn't make her go against her will. She finally recovered her thoughts, and we said our goodbyes.

Mrs. Patrick called me to tell me where she was leaving the keys to her house. Her son was driving in from New York, and then driving her across country to California, where she would live. That afternoon, I drove over to the house. Yes, the keys were there. But what else I found there shocked me! All the things she hadn't sold at her garage sale were at the curb. Apparently, her son pulled in, made no arrangements for any of these belongings, and shuffled her into his car for the very long cross country trip. As I entered the house and saw more articles left behind, I couldn't help but sob to myself. A lifetime of living was in this house, and this is what it's all about. As I opened drawers, and closets, I found a special decoration here, and a precious momento there, and so very many memories. All meaningless now, just left here to gather dust, wither away, just like that. I spent some time just going from room to room, thinking to myself, who would ever remember that an old woman lived here? Who would care?" It brought reality to me with a thud...this could be me at some time. Who is left to care for the old folks? What have we all accomplished in our lifetimes? Did we leave anything behind for future generations? Or is it just that we live, and then die. No, whether we be rich and famous, or the ordinary man, we all bring something to the table of life. And so, too, did Mrs. Patrick – whether it be in her years of teaching, or her years as a mom, or just her years as an old woman traveling to the unknown in her twilight years.

A Cry For Help
Grandpa's First Babysitting Job

E-Mail received early Monday morning from
Grandpa.

Maria, this is terrible. I don't think I can make it
until 5:30 tonight. Kevin is crying and he won't
listen to anything I say. I told Leela that I'm too
old for this. If I live to see the end of the day, I will
never baby-sit all day again. I don't think that I will
make it today. I'm going out of my mind with this
torture. If there is no answer to the door that
means that I had a heart attack. The key is in the
back of the house.

Tippy the Cat

I was afraid. My feline instincts told me everything I had known was gone. I was traveling down the paved street in a fast-moving car, and I had no idea where it was headed. What was to be my fate? There was a dark-haired woman steering and a bright-eyed little blond boy sitting next to her. He was cradling me in his arms, so that calmed me a little. He didn't act like he was going to hurt me.

Soon, we arrived at a simple house on a simple street. This little boy, Rocky was his name, eagerly carried me in and proudly displayed me to his dad. I still didn't know what this new adventure in my life would mean, but so far these strange people seemed to like me.

Next, I met a little girl about five years old, and she was really excited to see me, too. It seemed like this new family had adopted me and although I would miss my mother and siblings, the least I could do was try to accept my new situation.

Of course, I had to explore my new surroundings. I sniffed around all the rooms and found that there were two new bowls in the kitchen, one filled with water and the other with food. So, at least I wasn't going to starve. Now this family started to act a little silly – waving yarn in front of me and rolling balls past me. This was fun, though, and I enjoyed myself playing with all these new toys.

My first night loomed dark and ominous. Where was I expected to go? I soon had the answer to that question. Rocky scooped me upstairs and fluffed up a spot on his bed for me. Oh, how grand that felt. All warm and cuddly in the blankets with my new-found friend. He didn't forget me. He was really going to take care of me.

As the weeks went on, I became even more familiar with my surroundings. Wow, there was even a woods in back of the house. I had more fun hunting and stalking, and then stretching out in the hot sun to take nice long naps.

Rocky always had time for me. I loved him petting me and making a fuss over me. I remember one time I just wanted to get so close to him that I draped myself over his face. Life was good.

Along the way I had my first litter of kittens. It was a new experience and I hadn't really planned a birthplace for them. It was late at night when my first kitten arrived and since I just wanted to be close to Rocky, my friend, I had the kitten right on his bed. Rocky called out to everyone and they woke up and quickly prepared a box for the rest of my babies.

I had a second litter of kittens, but I remember the dark-haired lady crying when she had a hard time finding homes for my dear ones. After that, the lady took me on a short trip in that car again and left me with some people. I never had kittens again after that. Now, I really was afraid of those fast moving cars and taking trips!

Over the years, however, I was given so much love. Rocky, my friend, was really growing up. He was becoming a man. And pretty Linda was growing up, too.

Then one day, I could see Rocky running around in a dither. Some man was in the driveway waiting for him. They eventually left, together. I waited and waited, but Rocky didn't come home. Not for a week, or a month, or even many months. I made do with what was left. I even got up enough courage to go into the Family Room where I had very seldom ever gone. But the dark-haired lady allowed me to sneak up by the wall and leap over the back of the sofa into her arms. I heard her tell her husband that it was okay – that I was just lonely because Rocky had left. So, although I didn't see Rocky for a long time, I made adjustments and got to enjoy sleeping in the lady's lap. At night, I now slept with my friend Linda. She was so soft and kind and good to me. I think she understood.

I still enjoyed wandering in the woods, but now I was twelve years old and I preferred sleeping and lazing around. I reveled in the fact that I had people who loved me and I loved them, too. They were my family.

Soon, I did get to see Rocky again. He had been gone a really long time. I heard the family say he was in Germany, and in the Army. But, now he was coming home for thirty days. I was secretly looking forward to seeing him again. But, being a cat, I had to act aloof – that's the way of cats! When he arrived in the driveway, I just sauntered up to him, rubbed his leg, and allowed him to pet me. It wouldn't do for my dignity to let him know how very much I missed him and his gentle touch. So, for thirty days, Rocky loved me again. He'd run his fingers through my fur and call to me, "Tippy, guy, how's my cat?" I knew it was going to happen, and sure enough, off he went again, back to Germany. But I now knew that he'd be home for good in one more year. And I'd sure be here waiting for him. My old buddy from when I was just a youngster. He'd taken me through my youth, my adolescence, and now my adult life. What better friend could I ever want or have. My friend for life – Rocky.

The man and lady and pretty Linda just left in the car. Well, summer is drawing to an end and pretty soon I'll just stay in the house for the winter. The family always laughed about that – how after a certain date I wouldn't even set foot out of the warm, cozy house. So, this is one of my last chances to explore the neighborhood before holing up for the cold weather. I think I'll go across the street. I very rarely do that.

I had just started across the street when I looked up and saw one of those fast moving cars, and it was barreling right at me. God! How I wish I was as quick and agile as I was in my youth. But I

just can't seem to move fast enough, and HERE IT
COMES!

I am now laying in the middle of this hard,
cold street, and I feel my life ebbing out of me.
Where are my friends to hold me and love me.
Where is Rocky? There are some strange people
here, and they are kind. They have wrapped me in
a blanket and are softly speaking to me. Now, even
though my sight is blearing, I see my family's car
coming down the street. I hear pretty Linda
screaming. She's screaming for me! I'll try to hang
on until she can get to me. But I know I'll never
see my friend, Rocky. Everything is very dim now.
The light is leaving my body.

Rocky, my friend. I won't have time for that
one last goodbye. But my last thought is of the love
and affection you and your family bestowed on me.
I love you all. Goodbye.

Annulment

I CONCERNING YOUR COURTSHIP:

1. I grew up in Avon Lake. I lived in the same house, in the same neighborhood, and had the same friends from kindergarten through high school. I went to church with my mom. My dad was not Catholic so he did not attend. Our family consisted of mom, dad, older brother, and myself. My older brother and I were close. There was some tension in my home when I was growing up. My mother and father did not have the perfect marriage. There was frequent arguing. There were no illnesses, deaths, alcohol or drug abuse, emotional illnesses, or financial hardships. My mother did go to work soon after I started kindergarten. I remember this as distressing to me because I missed her not being there for me when I got home. My brother and I had the usual fights and quarrels, but I did enjoy a close relationship with him. I had the best friendships and these friendships have carried over to this day. My relationship with my parents is strong. They were always supportive of me.

2. My spouse grew up in a family consisting of mother, father, sister, brother, and himself. His relationship with his sister is very good. He has no relationship with his brother whatsoever. This brother never acknowledged me. If Paul and his brother are in the parents' house at the same time,

they do not acknowledge each other. I never found out why. His brother never attended our wedding. His dad seemed very condescending to his mother, and this bothered me quite a bit. He would belittle her in front of her relatives including her mother and father. I witnessed this, and it made me very uncomfortable. Paul told me when we were dating that he did not want a marriage like his parents. Paul said his father hit his mother at times, and because of this, he had nightmares. He told me that sometimes he felt his mom deserved it because she egged his dad on. Paul has a college education and a fine job as a teacher.

3. I met Paul on a blind date. He was attentive, he complimented me. We danced, he sang in my ear, and he made me feel special and beautiful.

4. We saw each other every day after we met. I remember going to meet his parents for the first time. Paul was rather rude to me and his parents had to make excuses for him. I felt very uncomfortable. Paul kept putting me on the spot at dinner. I thought maybe this was his way of teasing me. When we spent a weekend there, he would leave the room, not telling me where he was going, and I felt very uncomfortable staying up with his parents, because I did not know them very well yet. Several times in the beginning of our relationship, he yelled at me and I was embarrassed because we were at his parent's house.

5. We decided to marry 37 days after we met. We were then engaged for six months.

6. Before I met Paul, I had several steady, long-term relationships. In high school, I had two long-term dating relationships. In college, I dated two fellows and had a long-term relationship my last two years of college and into my first year out in the work force with a very nice person. I remain friends with these last two fellows to this day. Most of my dating was done on a long-term basis, always at least one year. With two of my boyfriends, the dating was three years. When I met Paul, I was 25 years old. I do not know much about Paul's dating habits. I believe that the last girl Paul had dated broke up with him because, as he told me, her mother stepped in and broke them up. He did not date anyone for some time until he met me.

7. Within three weeks of meeting Paul he wanted me to move in with him. He had purchased a house the previous year. I did not move in. Then, in another two weeks, he proposed marriage. He again insisted I move in with him. I was reluctant to do so before marriage, but did move in soon after the engagement. This was the first time I had ever lived with a boyfriend, but he was very insistent that I do so.

Everything happened very quickly then. Plans and preparations started for our wedding. Time seemed to fly. I knew that I wanted to put my touches on the house. There were some things I wanted to add. The house was rather stark, with bare walls and old furniture. However, I noticed that when I wanted to add something, it did not set well with Paul. I talked this over with some of my friends and mother, and we all seemed to feel that, of course, it was difficult for Paul to make changes because he had established his home on his own. Paul wanted me to start pooling my income, but I did not want to do so yet. I had debts that I wanted to take care of. I did not pool my income until a week before our marriage, because I didn't want to burden him with my debts after we got married. I had wanted to work over the summer (I was off all summer because I am a teacher) but he told me he would take care of me, that he wanted me with him, and that his food was my food, and all that he had was mine. So, I reluctantly quit my summer job. Paul wanted me at all his rehearsals for a community playhouse he was a part of. So, I attended these occasions and met many of his associates. Paul wanted me to be a complete part of his life.

In the middle of the summer, my brother, Jeff, and his wife, Laura, invited Paul and me up to Canada to vacation at my brother's father-in-law's cabin. So, Paul and I went there. Several things caught my attention. One night as we sat around a campfire singing, I noticed Paul with a very dark look on his face. I felt uncomfortable. I felt responsible for his well-being, and I asked him to join in on the fun. He replied that when he sang, he got paid for it. He wasn't going to sing for free. When everyone was singing, he kept saying his ears hurt because we weren't professional singers. He made some sarcastic comments about the fellow

121

playing the guitar. The host, my brother's father-in-law, is a podiatrist, and Paul made a comparison with podiatry and music. Paul said, "I'm not at work and therefore I won't sing." And then he said, "You don't see Laura's dad looking at everybody's feet." This attitude made me feel very bad and very apologetic for Paul's behavior. I felt especially bad for the family friend playing the guitar because Paul made hurtful comments to him.

Also, the next day, I was embarrassed because Paul went down to the lake and was about to take out our host's new boat, without first having asked permission. My brother stopped him, in a kindly manner and with a sense of humor, in order to remain friendly. Later in our relationship, Paul remarked that my brother was a "pompous ass."

Back at his house (Paul never really made me feel like it was my house, too) it was becoming a real ordeal to add decorations, a plant, pictures, etc. Paul almost always overruled me. No matter what I wanted to add, it was always a heart wrenching experience that led me to crying jags and frustration. Finally, Paul said I could add decorations to one of his bedrooms I did so, and I enjoyed doing it. However, eventually Paul took out my one main decorating item and said he needed it.

8. Our engagement was never broken. Once, I ran out of his house to my car, trying to get away from him and an argument, but he ran out and sat on the

hood of the car, blocking me from driving away. He said he would stay there until I came back in. I managed to pull out anyway.

9. Before marriage, we went through pre-Cana instruction. Paul thought this experience was stupid. I enjoyed it.

10. No problems with religion or the children being raised Catholic. Paul was a Catholic although he did not attend church regularly.

11. There were problems during the courtship and especially in the months before the wedding. I was told that these were not unusual – just wedding planning stress. Paul wanted me to give him my paychecks. His mother seemed to know more about me and my actions than I did myself. He told her some personal matters between the two of us that I felt should be just between the two of us. I was becoming rather surprised that his mother was so much a part of us. Paul was becoming more and more rude to my friends. He didn't even seem to be trying to be friendly to them.

12. Any doubts I had at this time I accounted to "wedding jitters." My parents did say that up to the moment I said "I do" I could walk away from getting married and not worry about any of the money being spent for the wedding. Inside, I felt that after we were married, things would be ok.

13. We were married. We had just one ceremony, a Catholic ceremony.

II CONCERNING THE MARRIAGE ITSELF:

14. On the wedding day, there were some conflicts. I recall leaving the church and doves were to be released. The owner of the doves came up and said he didn't realize the church had a cement overhang and he was concerned the doves could hit their heads on it when released, and die. He asked if we could come down the stairs to release the doves. Paul actually got very angry with the man and said, "No, we're going to do it the way I planned." I asked Paul to please come down the steps because I didn't want the doves to get hurt. Paul said no. He said he planned it this way and this is the way we're going to do it (release the doves from the top of the stairs).

On our wedding night, instead of getting romantic with me. Paul wanted to open all the wedding cards. Since we were school teachers and couldn't get away until December break for our honeymoon, we stayed at a motel that night. His parents stayed at a hotel nearby. I remember wanting to have a very romantic evening with him, including making love, and he didn't seem interested. Instead he called his mother at the nearby hotel and had her drop off all our wedding cards. So, instead of being romantic with me, Paul wanted to open all the wedding cards to see how much money we got. I remember regretfully going along with this because I didn't feel like I had any say in the matter. I had to beg him to consummate the marriage. And I cried, thinking to myself, 'Oh my God, whenever I dreamed of my wedding night, I imagined it being romantic and making love, and here I had to beg Paul to make love. So, we did.

We didn't go on our honeymoon until a month and a half later because we couldn't get time off from teaching until Christmas vacation. We went to Cancun. It was just awful. He didn't talk to me. He never smiled. It seemed like he was having a horrible time. I tried so hard to be lively and light-hearted, have fun, and try to make the best of it.

We joined an excursion one day to see the Mayan ruins and we were with the tour group. We all had to stay together and we were all talking. We came to an intersection and some of our group got through, but I stopped to let people pass by. But then Paul very harshly grabbed my arm and started to shove me through the intersection. And he loudly said, "We're NOT going to let them by." He said it loudly so that everyone in the group could hear. I was so embarrassed. Paul said, "No, we're staying with our group. We're not going to let them by." He shoved me through the group, shoved me along the trail, bumping me into the people so that we forced our way through this passing group. So then, very softly, I told him so that I wouldn't make a scene, "I was just trying to let them through. I don't know why you pushed me. That was kind of rude to those people." He just grabbed my arm and squeezed it and said "I'm

125

not going to get into this with you. We're here for a reason, and you're not going to ruin it for me." So I felt really bad because I wasn't trying to start an argument. I was just stopping to let people pass by. I didn't mean to get him mad at me.

For the rest of this excursion he would not let me get two inches away from him and he let everyone know it. He literally was dragging me. He had my arm in a lock behind me like I was a prisoner, just like policemen take criminals. The entire day went that way. On the bus ride back to our room I was so upset I couldn't talk. I was so embarrassed that our tour group heard the ugly remarks Paul made and saw how he was treating me.

We got to our room and I said to him, "I just don't understand. We're on our honeymoon and I don't know why you would treat me that way in front of all those people who we had to be with all day." I felt very much like an animal. He made me feel like an animal. So, I got very upset and I was crying and crying very hard. And I told him I was going to go for a walk because I needed to be by myself. He restrained me by putting my hands behind my back and holding them there and then he mightily smacked me across the face and the impact knocked me to the floor. It hurt and stung terribly. Then I remember sobbing and I felt like I was hallucinating. I felt my whole world crash in on me that my husband would inflict such harm on me. I cried and said I wanted a divorce. I told him that there was no way I could live my life with a man who was capable of treating me in such a horrible way. All my life I never dreamed that my marriage would be like that. I was married for life and I didn't understand why my life was turning out like that.

15. At the time, I thought we were entering the marriage with mutual love.

16. The marriage was consummated on our wedding night, although I had to be the instigator, and throughout the marriage I had to beg Paul for intimacy. During the course of the five months we were together in the marriage, we had sex three to four times. I cried every morning when he would get out of bed. He never cuddled me, kissed me, or showed any affection. At the very beginning of our courtship, he wooed me and it was the best courtship. He was a gentleman, romantic, loving and affectionate. As our courtship went on, there was less and less of this side of Paul, but I continued to only see that good side of him because I didn't want to see and admit that our relationship wasn't the same as when we had first met.

After the marriage ceremony, the deterioration in our relationship worsened. I thought after the ceremony he would be the way he was in the early days of our courtship. However, now he barely talked to me. I remember one night we had a fight because, as we were driving to a video rental store, he changed stations on my car radio. I loved the song on the station he was switching from, but he became irate that I even asked him to keep my station on. So then, he set all dials to that one station he wanted. I got upset because I would have to re-program all my stations again. I didn't want to go into the video store with him. He went into the store. He was confident I would just stay there because he had the car keys. (However, I had learned by this time to always have an extra house key and car key). I drove off and left him at the video store. I drove around the block twice, for what felt like ten minutes, then went back to the store. He was gone, already, though. I assumed that he had a friend pick him up. I even went into the store. But he wasn't there.

I got home before him. He came in about an hour later. He came in the door. I sat there. I was afraid as to what he might do. I was on the couch. First, he didn't talk to me for about ten minutes. I just sat there on the couch waiting, because I knew something was going to happen. He started to yell at me. "How dare I! and that I was a bitch. He pinned me down on the couch very forcefully. He tried to tear my shirt off. He laid on me so hard and he had my hands pinned behind me on the couch. Paul said that he was going to F--- me so that he could impregnate me and I wouldn't leave. He literally ripped my shirt off me. He was trying to pull my pants down. All the while he was shouting in my face, yelling, and spittle was spewing out of his mouth. He was screaming "F--- this and "F--- that. I'm going to impregnate you whether you want to or not." And

I was crying and begging for mercy. I kept pleading with him saying this isn't how it's supposed to be.

I had already decided I was going to leave him that weekend. In that past month, I had made sure that I was doing nothing wrong in the marriage. I was being kind and nice. It didn't work, though. He still wouldn't talk to me. He put down everything I did and wouldn't do anything with me, like a walk in the park, which I liked to do. I always had to be at his play practice so I could watch him. We were in bed and I said, "You know, I've been nice to you and I don't see what I have been doing wrong for you to treat me this way. I feel like I'm not even a part of this marriage, like I'm invisible. I can't believe that you haven't thought about leaving me. Have you thought about divorce?" And he said, "I don't want a divorce. I can just get a mistress." And then he said, "Remember, I've made many women cum in this bed."

During the four months we were together in the marriage, sexual relations occurred just three to four times. He complained and said that his penis hurt. That sex hurt him. He called his mother every day and told her what I had done that day. He would do this in front of me and I would be distressed that he would tell his mother such details about me.

17. The marriage was contracted freely. No force on either side.

18. We intended a permanent binding union.

19. We discussed names for children, but nothing in detail as to how to raise children.

20. No children were born.

21. No children were born because the marriage lasted less than six months. I did nothing to prevent conception, but probably because we only had relations three to four times, the likelihood just wasn't there.

22. We both intended to be faithful. We had no specific philosophy regarding being faithful.

23. During the marriage, we were both faithful to each other.

24. Before our marriage, I was becoming very concerned about how our relationship was deteriorating but I wrote it all off because I felt we were stressed in planning our big wedding.

III TERMINATION OF MARRIAGE:

25. I lived in Avon Lake. Paul lived in Elyria. We had no children, no separations during the marriage. We met in April, got engaged in May, and married in November. Then we had a delayed honeymoon at Christmas time. I sought counseling in February. My counselor was afraid for me. I sought the counseling for my own mental state of mind. I finally broke down and confided in my

best friends. I had not confided the problems in my marriage to anyone because I did not want them to think badly of my husband. My counselor felt very strongly that I should get out of the house, and the marriage, immediately. Yet, the counselor also wanted to give Paul a chance to come in for counseling. I told Paul that I had seen a counselor and that the counselor recommended that Paul come in with me next time. Paul outright refused and said, "I am not seeing a f------ counselor with you." I left in March. Our dissolution was in June.

26. We had problems from day 1 of the marriage – the restraining, the controlling. From day 1, he called his mother daily to report my actions, and he would do this in front of me. I was embarrassed that he would tell his mother some of the most private details of our marriage. He told her that he had slapped me on our honeymoon, even.

On a typical day, I would wake up. He was still in bed. I would leave early and work all day. When I came home, I cooked supper. He would be late because of practice, etc. We would sit down and eat and he would not say anything to me. No talk whatsoever. I tried to talk and his answers would be just one word or a grunt. I was restrained at least once a day. He would lock me in the bedroom, even for little things and wouldn't let me go to the bathroom without him going with me and watching me to be sure I wasn't out of his sight. He didn't want me to leave the house so he would do everything possible to keep me there. I would start to lock myself in the bathroom to get away

131

from him restraining me. That's when he took the lock off the bathroom door so I couldn't get away from him. If I would want to get away from him, he would hold me in a headlock on the floor so I couldn't move. I would want to get away and he would keep me there for as long as fifteen minutes. He would say "I'm not letting you go." When I would beg to be released, he would laugh in my face, while I was crying. Then I would beg to go to the bathroom, because that's how I would try to get away. After he took the lock off the door, he would insist on watching me go the bathroom to be sure I wasn't lying about having to go, and not just saying that to get away from him. He would also lock me in the bedroom, mainly for the same reasons. So I couldn't get away from him. He started to hide my car keys so I couldn't leave the house. That was when I first decided to always have duplicate keys.

Most evenings ended with us watching television and at bedtime there would be no romantic overtures. We went to bed at the same time. He would immediately go to sleep. On the occasions when we did visit or see people, he would be rude to me. If it were my friends he would be rude to them. If it were his friends, he liked to be the center of attention.

27. Immediately, problems in communications arose. He wouldn't talk. He said he wasn't interested in what happened to me in my day at school. Financially I turned my check over to Paul and he charged me my half of the house payment,

utilities, and half of everything else. He did not want to include payments to my mother on some money I owed her. He felt she should just forgive the debt. He did not ever mention taking the house out of his mother's and his name, and adding me. The house title remained in their names only. In the marriage, there was much verbal and physical abuse. It only worsened each day that the marriage went on. These issues were never resolved. They accelerated.

28. My main complaint is as a husband Paul broke down my self-esteem, embarrassed and ridiculed me in front of my family and friends. He would call my mother, or a friend, and tell them the things I did wrong, and try to win them over to him.

29. Paul complained that I never went to watch him at his play practices. He wanted me to sit there and watch him for three hours, once a week. This was a big complaint of his.

30. We lived together for five months before the marriage, and four months into the marriage.

31. There were no separations. Only the final leaving. My counselor strongly suggested that I get out. My counselor told me under no circumstances to stay in that house with Paul. No matter how minor or major, one more thing happening in that house, he told me to get out. He told me he would prefer that I never go back. But he knew that I needed to make sure I was making the right decision, because it was hard for me to leave. So

the counselor said give him one more chance, more for my own sake then the counselor's sake. But professionally he had to suggest and recommend that Paul come back with me for a visit.

I also met with the deacon who married me. He told me that professionally he would recommend Paul and I talk it out and see a counselor together, but as my friend, he told me I did the right thing in leaving and that I shouldn't go back.

32. No.

33. No.

34. In Cancun, after he slapped me, I said I would have to divorce him.

35. I did seek counseling. I offered Paul the opportunity to also go, but he refused. I continued to see the counselor for over a year to recuperate from the devastation of the marriage and the abuse.

36. I initiated the divorce proceeding and I paid for the entire process. I could not endure the marriage any longer.

37. Based on my discussion with my deacon, I finally viewed this as the only possible course of action.

38. No children

IV REGARDING THE CHARACTER AND PERSONALITY OF YOUR SPOUSE:

39. Before marriage, Paul was like a man in a romantic movie. He was attentive, romantic, and seemed to have my best interests at heart.

40. Before the marriage, there were signs of emotional imbalances. For instance, he related to me how he dreamt that his father slit his mother's throat. He mentioned many times how his father hit his mother. His brother did not speak to him at all.

41. He never underwent any psychiatric, psychological, or professional help.

42. I would say Paul seemed ready for marriage in terms of being settled in his career and established in his life. I felt he was mature and ready for marriage.

43. I have not seen Paul since the dissolution of the marriage.

V REGARDING YOUR OWN CHARACTER AND PERSONALITY:

44. I am basically a polite individual, caring of others, and empathetic.

45. No mental, emotional, or nervous disorders before my marriage. I experienced emotional problems during and after the marriage. Self-

esteem, security, my mental health, all these I felt were being destroyed.

46. I saw a counselor during the last months of my marriage.

47. When I reflect back, yes, I feel I was ready for marriage. I was established in my career, I was of a mature age. No, I did not exercise good judgment and I was too willing to chalk everything up to wedding jitters. Lurking in the back of my mind however, was a disturbing thought that the bad things that were happening might get worse. I did feel though, that the marriage would be okay after the ceremony. I thought things would get a lot better because we were fighting about the wedding plans. We had problems agreeing on music, programs, etc. I felt that after the ceremony, we wouldn't have these things to argue about any longer.

48. Presently, I am in a great frame of mind. It took me over a year to recover from the low points of my marriage, and the abuse in the marriage.

Poetry for a Rainy Day

To all our Moms…..

The thread of life weaves through the sun's rays,
Showering the land with glorious days,
And the graceful beauty of its soft light
Spreads through the land in a wondrous delight.

God made this awesome beauty for all
For you and for me and for one and for all.
But wait, he did not stop, there's more.
He looked around and found a door.

And through this door walked endless love
And courage and strength and hope from above.
Who was this creation? And what was she called?
Why, simply mother, and we are enthralled.

We are blessed and we are united,
All of us, for our most delighted.
Who gave us the guidance and patience needed
To forge ahead with life, unheeded.

She tended our wounds and bruises and souls
And instilled in us our future goals.
She gave us breath to forge ahead
Into jobs or careers or wherever life led.

Her gentle feet on the sands of time
Gave meaning to her own sweet rhyme.
The love and nurturing she bestowed on us
Gave us a feeling of sheer tenderness.

And when we were able to stand tall and straight
God opened the heavens to his pearly gate.
He called out to our mother, "Come walk with
thee,
Sit by my side and be with me."

Through the mists of time and softness tender
Our mom did travel to a land of splendor.
God drew her near and the heavens glowed
In the glorious might of her heavenly abode.

Now we are left with the most wonderful story
Of our mom's sweetest gifts and heavenly glory.
Thus to this end we will kneel and pray
With her in our hearts, forever, to stay.

Duke
Dedicated to Rocco Satullo

The college kid, Rocky, happy in thought
Books and notes scattered about
Yet something missing in all the mess
A certain sadness and dreariness.

What lacked? What was fittin?
Why of course! A cat! A kitten!
That very day, the search began
By reading the ads from the newspaperman.

The perfect ad began his search
And there he drove, without a lurch
There's one, all brown and gray and white
All said and done, a perfect sight!

And so it came that Duke was my name
I was loved and petted and pampered and tamed
I had the run of the house by day
And could romp in the yard in wild play!

But one sad day, I was found by the street
Limp and haggard, and dirty and beat.
What caused this horrible chain of events?
It did not make any kind of sense!

Hit by a car! Left for dead!
What an awful fate! What an awful dread!
Rushed to the vet, the verdict was made
I would survive, I would not fade!

As time went on Rocco took Becky, his wife

And together they forged a really good life.
I settled in to play in the house
And had fun looking for that evasive mouse.

Children expanded the family to four
And a big, new house let me explore
Out in the yard, the fields, the woods,
Where I could hunt for the best of the goods

Oh! How carefree and happy and sweet
My days were fun and utterly complete
Bask in the sun, or lie in wait
Or run with the children to the garden gate

Year after year brought joys and fun
And winter grays and summer suns
I relished it all but as of late
Can't help but dwell on my impending fate

Tired in body and slow in gait
Is not my usual, daily trait
But my body is heavy and my eyes barely see
And everyone has to keep tending me.

I lay in soft grass and see the frogs leaping
I can even hear the cars endless beeping.
But my body betrays me, my fur is all matted,
My bones are all brittle, my mind is so tattered.

Daylight is faltering, nights are so long
Life just keeps playing its own silent song
Please, my dear family, no sadness, no tears
Just lie down beside me and put out my fears

Remember the good times, the playing, the joy
And all the memories of your girl and your boy
All of us romping across the back lawn
Everything so right, and nothing so wrong.

As dimness increases, and my mind becomes light
I look up at Rocky, what a wondrous sight!
You have made my life such a blaze of glory
And allowed me to have such a wonderful story.

Now as I close my eyes and lay back my head
I silently ask that no tears should be shed
I have been petted and loved and treated with care
No more could I ask for in my final soft prayer.

Precious Mayapple
Dedicated to Doug and Paula Criswell

It's cold up here on the mountain
Especially so at night,
But I pray I may be rescued
I pray with all my might.

I feel so lost and abandoned
Can no one see my plight?
I'll snuggle in the bushes
Until daytime comes to light.

I hear the roar of an engine
Of a motorcycle ride.
Now it pulls to the side of the road,
So close to where I hide.

Straggly, am I, and wary,
Yet could this be my friend?
He approaches with a hand out,
My message I will send.

Yes, pick me up and love me,
And I will love you to the end.
Both you and the lovely lady
Who stands around the bend.

Now racing on the highway,
What a sight to see,
I'm in some crazy structure,
There's Doug and Paula, and me.

Lo' our destination is reached
And what a bliss I'm in
With warmth and food and care
Away from all the din.

Now surprise to all
I am about to lay in birth
Of just one tiny kitten
Who will join me on this earth.

Lovely days, months, years
Pass in such a pleasure
With the love of Doug and Paula
To last me now and forever.

But wait! What is forgotten
Is that time is brief and short
We cannot walk forever
On the pebbles of our court.

My body will betray me
And weaken with dismay
And finally I'll take that walk
That will steal me away.

Away from love and laughter
And days and nights of glee,
Where I merrily spent my days
In splendid love with thee.

Goodbye to my protectors
Who muffle their soft cry.
And now I lay my head down,
And say goodbye, and die.

Sylvie
Dedicated to Linda Barlock

The alley is bleak and dark
And the night is very black,
I'm wandering all alone
With a great fear at my back.

How did I happen to come to this?
To be so cast aside,
I feel so rejected
No love, no hope, no pride.

There is no human being
To stay and be my guide.
I've had to be so stoic
And take it all in stride.

I'm just a castaway cat
Who is trying to make my way.
Is there no one at all
With whom I can ultimately stay?

The cat lady dutifully comes
On her nightly mercy mission
And bends and scoops me up,
She needs no one's permission.

Then comes lady Linda
With her arms open wide.
She welcomes me so completely,
I no longer need to hide.

The days, the months, the years
Run fast and true and sure
From college to work to marriage
I just want to be with her.

Enriching love and caring
Warmth and fun and laughter
Now fill all my days
Today and forever after.

But as it is in all matters
Time can be a friend
Or a fierce and ugly monster
Not willing to bow or bend.

Where now is my youth?
My speed and style and grace?
It's all left – gone – behind me,
In some other time and place.

Now in my frailty and weakness
And as darkness dares comes near,
I am in such a wonderment
That Linda sheds a tear.

I love you so much, sweet Linda
Love you like no other
And as I pass, from this my life,
Have no regrets to smother.

You gave me all I needed
That and then some more.
Don't think for even a minute
That you failed in any score.

Although you may not see it, my lovely Linda lady,
You did your utmost best.
Now let me lay my head down
In quiet, final rest.

Your love was always there for me
From the reaches of your heart,
And that's what really mattered
When it came the time to part.

My Beloved Pat
Dedicated to Marcia Lapp

Don't know how I got here
Don't know where I'm at
I'm searching for a home
I'm just a lonely cat.

Up ahead I see a place
Shining in the sun
I'll take a chance and go right up
Can this be the one?

I break into a run with haste
Across the plush green lawn
Hoping that the owner
Will not be away! All Gone!

I meow a little by the door
With my own special sound
Then wait with great hope
As the owner comes 'round.

In a moment surprise!
A young woman steps out
She looks down and sees me
But seems in such doubt.

Then slowly she stoops
And sees I'm no threat.
She leans down to get me
To make me her pet.

Oh! The pleasure of food
And comfort of bed
It can never be better
I'm warm and all fed.

The freedom to run
Roam and explore
Leads me to yards
Of neighbors galore.

Then soon, a friend,
Another lost cat
Comes into the home
To love and to pat.

Rudy and me,
We make such a team
As I rule the house
And let off my steam.

While Rudy chooses
To hide under the bed
Ha Ha! I'm Alpha cat
There, it's been said!

Our owner, sweet Marcia
Loves us so much
Enjoys all our antics
And we love her touch.

Time, and time, passes
And I feel great
But wait! Something's amiss
Is this called fate?

149

My dear friend Marcia
Sees me on the floor
I'm having trouble breathing
I'm rasping and feel sore.

Her lovely hands wrap round me
And take me to the car
We're in a little room now
But Marcia is not far.

I know that I am dying
And everything's a blur
But I hear her words of love,
As she soothes my coat of fur.

Green fields are all about me
As I fall into a sleep
Please my dearest Marcia
Do not sit down and weep.

For you have given life to me
When I showed up at your door
And lavished me with love
And OH! OH! So much more.

Remember all the fun we had
Don't dwell on this, my leaving
Take heart, my love at this sad time
I do not want you grieving.

About The Author

Kathleen LaRocque Satullo grew up in Cleveland, Ohio and as a newlywed moved to Avon Lake, Ohio where she raised her family. She spent her early working years as an Administrative Assistant, finally becoming a Realtor in 1987. You can visit her at <u>katsat2005@yahoo.com</u> if you, too, have a sob story.